MW00974348

Half-Truths
Are Lies

Half-Truths
Are Lies

Thomas P. Dooley, Ph. D.

HIGHLAND PARK, ILLINOIS

© Copyright 2009 – Thomas P. Dooley, Ph.D.

Printed in the United States of America

Published by:
Mall Publishing Company
641 Homewood Avenue
Highland Park, Illinois 60035
877.203.2453

Cover Design by Andrew Ostrowski
Text Design by Marlon B. Villadiego

All rights reserved. This book is protected by the copyright laws of the United States of America. This book may not be copied or reprinted for commercial gain or profit. The use of short quotations or occasional page copying for personal or group study is permitted and encouraged. Permission will be granted upon request.

Unless otherwise identified, Scripture is taken from the HOLY BIBLE: NEW INTERNATIONAL VERSION˚. NIV˚. Copyright © 1973, 1978, 1984 by International Bible Society. Used by permission of Zondervan. The "NIV" and "New International Version" trademarks are registered in the United States Patent and Trademark Office by International Bible Society.

Certain pronouns in Scripture that refer to the Father, Son, and Holy Spirit may be capitalized and may differ from some Bible publishers' styles.

ISBN 1-934165-35-2

Path Clearer, Inc.
PO Box 661466
Birmingham, Alabama
35266-1466 USA
info@pathclearer.com
www.pathclearer.com

ENDORSEMENTS

Failure to balance your car wheels could prove disastrous. The faster you accelerate the greater potential for trouble. The Church likewise is heading for disaster if she continues to promote many of her current popular teachings. God warns us in His Word that, *"a false balance is an abomination to the Lord"*. This pertains not only to weights and measures but also to Biblical truth, or as author, Tom Dooley, refers to them as *Half-Truths*. This book is long overdue and provides the vital antidote for the poison that many have swallowed under the label of truth. Immerse yourself in this wealth of wisdom. It could save you from serious deception and its deadly consequences.

David Ravenhill, *Author of "Surviving the Anointing" and Itinerant Speaker; Siloam Springs, Arkansas*

Dr. Dooley exposes the truth about the lies people believe. Many people are living in a time where performance is more valued that what Scripture states. This is a much needed and refreshing book to expand our understanding of The Truth.

Robert McGee, *Author of "The Search for Significance", Counselor, and Itinerant Speaker; Jacksonville, Florida*

America is facing God's judgments today. Hopefully they are remedial and will lead to repentance in Church, and awakening in the nation. If the Bible is true, and it is, and we do not return to God, His remedial judgments will become final judgments and America, whether slowly or swiftly, will be destroyed (Psalm 9:17). Tom Dooley exposes the lies and false doctrines we have believed that have kept us from knowing God in both His goodness and severity (Romans 11:22). We in America and the decadent West have little time to take to heart the truths Dr. Dooley has made plain in *Half-Truths are Lies*. As he suggests, the truths in Rev. Jonathan Edwards sermons that sparked the first Great Awakening, are the very truths America must embrace today. May God have mercy and may preachers and laymen alike, read, believe and act upon the truths in this book.

Rev. Pierre Bynum, *Chaplain and National Prayer Director of the Family Research Council; Washington, DC*

As I read your book, I had a vision of a courtroom in which the Church was being brought to trial. Jesus turned to those who claimed to know and love Him, held out a Bible and said, *"Do you swear to tell the truth, the whole truth and nothing but the truth, so help you God"!* There was stunned silence because the "Church" would not lay its hand on the Word of God. Why? It is because we are to be the true witnesses of the Gospel with no compromise concerning its truth, but because of the lust of the flesh, the lust of the eyes and the pride of life (1 John 2:16) so many who should be proclaiming the truth of the Gospel have become snared by the master of lies and half truths, Satan himself. Thank you Tom for this book. It is so timely and desperately needed. Let its truth be shouted from the rooftops. I will gladly climb up there with you and help you shout.

Dee Baxter, *President of Baxter Bible Ministries; LaFayette, Georgia*

What a timely message from a true prophet of God. *Half-Truths are Lies* is a hard-hitting expose' of our times in the world economy and exposes many, so-called, Christian organizations for what they have become. Worldly values and social expectations have permeated and tainted some work of the church. These men and women have become so "results" oriented that they have forgotten to know Him and to love Him. Dr. Dooley uses the Holy Scriptures to call attention to the blight that has nearly overtaken some ministries and is consuming our world. Ministries, knowingly or unknowingly, become self-destructive or limit themselves. Thank God, for this clear call to Biblical character and integrity that is such a foundational portion of the Kingdom.

Ray S. Phipps, *Ed.D., CEO of Bible Living Ministries, Inc.;*
Rapid City, South Dakota

God warns us over and over in His Word about false prophets and false teachers. *Half-Truths are Lies* exposes these modern day charlatans for what they are. Tom Dooley's gift of prophecy comes across boldly and clearly in his latest book. This is a "must read" for all evangelical vocational pastors. Hopefully, God's true prophets and teachers will read this book, study God's Word, preach and teach His truths boldly and focus on making disciples of all nations.

Royce L. Watkins, *CEO of Cebert Pharmaceuticals;*
Birmingham, Alabama

"The time will come when they will not endure sound doctrine; but wanting to have their ears tickled, they will accumulate for themselves teachers in accordance to their own desires; and will turn away their ears from the truth, and will turn aside to myths." (2 Timothy 4:3-4, NASB). Those discerning among us have realized that this "time" has "come". The present pattern, in which seminarians are growing mega-churches through the employ of a formulaic and humanistic church-growth philosophy, should raise red flags to authentic Church leadership far and wide. For the spirit fueling such "growth" often masks itself handsomely in half-truths. I commend Tom Dooley for taking a very unpopular prophetic posture in this hour, and for speaking whole-truths.

David Davenport, *Itinerant Minister, The Quiet Corner;*
Somerville, Ohio

I compliment you on your new book, and for exposing the current fallacies in the prosperity messages. After almost thirty years of teaching the word of God, I have found that only a very few people will research the Word of God for the truth. In addition, the message that God is in all things, both good and bad, is a hard truth for most Christians today. This truth has been one of the major issues that has cost me friends, church members, and much rejection over the years. Thank you for having the courage to put in print these truths that will surely bless the *Remnant* – those who have a heart after truth and have discarded personal agenda.

Rev. Don Brown, *Pastor of Living Waters Church;*
Chelsea, Alabama

Half-Truths are Lies is a breath of fresh air! Tom Dooley has taken the bold step of revealing the lies behind the modern Western church's Prosperity Gospel while, at the same time, presenting a balanced understanding of God's sovereign holiness and use of personal trials to lovingly shape and mould us.

> **Don Carmichael**, *President of Champion Events Group;*
> *Birmingham, Alabama*

Tom has a desire to encourage and support bi-vocational ministries. The timing of the teachings within this book is in line with what God seems to be doing today with marketplace ministry. There are gifts within business-men besides financial resources that are not being appreciated and utilized by local churches. God has used shoe cobblers to become Missionaries and has used fishermen and tent makers to become Evangelists and Apostles. I believe that Tom is right -- God still wants to use marketplace, bi-vocational men and women today to minister His Life to the Body.

> **William (Gene) Cary**, *CEO of Southern Store Fixtures;*
> *Birmingham, Alabama*

From the beginning, the devil has challenged God's words by attempting to alter the meaning of what the Lord intended. These deceptive strategies are still at work today. The Lord is calling His people to be seekers of truth in this hour. Tom Dooley is seeking to draw us back to the truth of God's Word. While reading this book, you may not easily agree with what is presented, but you will be challenged to search the Scriptures for yourself - which in my opinion is the point.

> **Ben Dixon,** *Director of 11th Hour Ministries;*
> *Lynnwood, Washington*

There are times when God puts a book into the hands of men and women intended to be used as a plumb line. Such a book is the one you hold in your hands. My good friend Tom Dooley has crafted another book that is provocative, yet palatable to the "contrite in spirit". In my humble estimation, its greatest contribution is that it is sacrilegious towards "icons" of contemporary doctrines that have failed the plumb line test. Read it. Repent. Be refreshed!

Brian Francis Hume, *Itinerant prophetic minister;*
Fredericksburg, Virginia

Half-truths are Lies is a testimony that is trustworthy and true. In it, Tom Dooley has placed his hand on Scripture, raised his right hand, and sworn to tell the truth -- the whole truth -- and nothing but the truth, so help him God.

Greg Reagan, *Certified Public Accountant;*
Birmingham, Alabama

People are always suggesting that I read a book they have just finished on a given topic. My response is always the same. "Who wrote it?" For most people, knowing who the author is validates the content. If the author has proven their credentials (in all but exceptional circumstances), then you can trust the content. I endorse Tom Dooley as a trustworthy man whose credentials and writings can be trusted.

Rev. Paul S Griffiths, *Pastor Kirkby Baptist Church;*
Liverpool, England

TABLE OF CONTENTS

ACKNOWLEDGMENTS

I am grateful for the revelation and knowledge given to me by Yahweh, which in part has been incorporated into this book.

I am grateful for the love and grace of the Lord shown to me through my lovely wife, Laura. She has the gifts of compassion, helps, and mercy and effectively uses these virtues to balance and temper the prophetic voice within me.

I am grateful to my long-term closest friends -- John Manwell, Paul Dewees, and Paul Griffiths, to whom I am routinely accountable concerning my words and deeds. We've remained loyal friends and colleagues for decades. These three mature brothers in Christ in addition to Melvin Slotnick and Don Stewart and other Path Clearer Board Members provide encouragement, exhortation, and occasional course correction.

I am grateful for the friendship with Howard Morgan and especially his teachings on the themes of the Kingdom of God, Hebraic Roots of the Judeo-Christian faith, and Apostolic-Prophetic ministry.

I am grateful to Don Carmichael for providing some editorial assistance with the final draft.

I am grateful to the *Remnant*, to the *Obedient*, to the *Righteous*, to the *Disciples*, to the *Called-Out Ones*, and to the genuine *Prophetic Voices* who reliably speak the truth-in-love!

PART I
Self-Serving Ministries

I know your deeds; you have a reputation of being alive, but you are dead.
Wake up! Strengthen what remains and is about to die, for I have not found
your deeds complete in the sight of my God. (Revelation 3:1a-2)

The purpose of this work is to deal head-on with some popular beliefs and teachings of contemporary Christian theology that need to be seriously reevaluated and corrected, as they are negatively affecting individuals, churches and ministries, as well as society. In essence, this book is a call to repentance – a long overdue and serious need for a change of mindset and of actions.

As an author and international speaker, I do not sugar coat Biblical truths, even if they are not politically correct. I do not agree with religious ecumenicalism where essential Biblical truths are compromised for the sake of tolerance or for tickling someone's ears with pleasant words. As disciples of Jesus we are to be tolerant in a general sense of people and issues that stretch beyond our cultural norms. We are to demonstrate understanding and compassion toward the disparate perspectives of others. But, we are not to be tolerant of sin in any form! A Biblical worldview demands that of us. With regard to sin *per se*, we must remain "narrow-minded." We are to love that which God loves and to hate that which He hates. We are commanded to *"…Hate what is evil; cling to what is good."* (Romans 12:9b). This instruction isn't popular in many circles these days. But it is honoring to God's Biblical revelation and His desires for us.

I seek to be a prophetic voice of *truth-in-love* and choose to use tough words whenever necessary. It is high time that someone shares the following insights in a clear presentation. At times criticism is needed. And this is one of those times as many – if not most – people are losing their compass bearings. These aberrant beliefs are not just affecting the self-declared Christians, they are also affecting all of society. Our Western watered-down "Christianity" is missing the mark.

Much of what transpires in Christendom today has little to do with a Biblical worldview. It has become popular to just select the pleasant things you want to believe from a menu of many options, like surfing the Internet or using a TV remote control. But a worldview that is built upon a foundation of sand will not prevail. A religious-philosophical values system that is built on a faulty foundation of *half-truths* and presumptions will not be sufficient.

Therefore, let us take a hard look at some of the trendy theological concepts that are based upon *half-truths*. In particular, the emphasis in this first section is on what's wrong with many churches and ministries… perhaps not all, but certainly many. If one were given the task of cataloging all of the common problems within churches and ministries, it would take hundreds of volumes to elaborate each of the issues. Represented in this book are several of the most grievous issues of our day affecting many churches and ministries, with an enhanced emphasis placed squarely on the leadership of those specific organizations.

With the overwhelming greed and corruption on Wall Street, the errors of *Prosperity Theology* in pulpits and on so-called "Christian TV" programs, and the self-serving false prophetic voices who tickle ears with only pleasant words, let's contemplate the parallel warnings from the prophet Micah. He summarized their former situation that closely parallels our current blights: "*As for the prophets who lead my people astray, if one feeds them, they proclaim 'peace'; if he does not, they prepare to wage war against him…*[and referring to Israel and Judah] *Her leaders judge for a bribe, her priests teach for a price, and her prophets tell fortunes for money. Yet they lean upon the LORD and say, 'Is not the LORD among us? No disaster will come upon us.'"* (Micah 3:7,11; emphasis added). Blatant disregard for God's revealed truth, in Micah's particular case for the sake of making a buck, was appalling to the genuine prophets back then. It is still appalling to genuine prophetic voices today. Blatant disregard for the word of God was common back then; for instance, consider King Jehoiakim, who cut up the prophetic warnings of Jeremiah and tossed them into the fire (Jeremiah 36). Unfortunately, blatant disregard for God's words is ever so common today. We just pick and choose what sounds nice to us.

Half-Truths are Lies was written in view of these common theological errors in order to be a clarion call for us to <u>wake up</u>! Let us embrace the *Whole Counsel of the LORD*. May the Lord give us the grace to wade through these issues as we consider them from a fresh perspective. Portions of this book will be highly provocative to many of us. That is precisely why it was written!

"The prudent see danger and take refuge, but the simple keep going and suffer for it." (Proverbs 27:12). I am just a messenger sounding the warning alarm about some of the insidious dangers in contemporary theology. It is my prayer that God give to each of us the *"spirit of wisdom and revelation that we might know Him better"* (Ephesians 1:17).

1

Right on the Money!

~

"Watch out! Be on your guard against all kinds of greed; a man's life does not consist in the abundance of his possessions." (Luke 12:15)

This chapter is written in order to expose a common theological ideology that is based upon a Biblical *half-truth*. It is commonly referred to as *Prosperity Theology*. Because it is only partially true, the teachings and behaviors associated with it are an admixture of good and bad principles. This is a particularly sticky issue of contemporary theology that impacts negatively on our lives as disciples of Jesus as well as on society in general.

Money is a common source of disappointments, greed, crime, and marital problems. The lack of money and the growth of debt can lead to hopelessness. Our Western culture has placed expectations on each of us to prosper beyond our means to provide for ourselves. We are ravenous wolves seeking more money and more possessions. *"Whoever loves money never has money enough; whoever loves wealth is never satisfied with his income. This too is meaningless. As goods increase, so do those who consume them. And what benefit are they to the owner except to feast his eyes on them?"* (Ecclesiastes 5:10-11).

A focus on financial prosperity and leisure have contributed toward de-emphasizing the Biblical values of discipline, righteous living, suffering, the consequences of sin, and the overriding sovereignty of the Almighty. Like it or not, the West's growing addiction to financial prosperity and materialism is negatively influencing our worldview and collective theology. Jesus declared, "*No servant can serve two masters. Either he will hate the one and love the other, or he will be devoted to the one and despise the other. You cannot serve both God and Money.' The Pharisees, who loved money, heard all this and were sneering at Jesus. He said to them, 'You are the ones who justify yourselves in the eyes of men, but God knows your hearts. What is highly valued among men is detestable in God's sight.'*" (Luke 16:13-15; emphasis added). The love of money brought out fierce judgment by Jesus.

As the colloquial saying goes, we need to get *"Right on the Money!"* One clear ramification is the growth of material prosperity's religious offspring – *Prosperity Theology* that is associated with many televangelists (typically Charismatic or Pentecostal in persuasion) and their close cousins occupying pulpits and positions of leadership in various ministries. Many of the proponents of *Prosperity Theology* are compelled to collect as much wealth for themselves as possible to justify their errant view that financial wealth equates with the "blessings of God". To them, affluence is a requirement of being a preacher of this "new" affluence message. However, it lacks Biblical accountability to the *whole* truth. This "new" theology is difficult to defend if one is honest with the *Whole Counsel of the LORD* in Scripture, unless one picks and chooses only the nice "positive" verses of the Bible to support it.

In many facets of life we must stay centered on the road and avoid the ditches on either side. If we err too much to the left we will fall into that ditch. And if we err too much to the right we will fall into the other ditch. God has established many truths in the Bible that seem to have apparent contradictions going in opposite directions. To deny "half" of the Biblical truths on an issue will result in us falling into one of the two opposing philosophical ditches. Denial or suppression of half of the truth leaves us believing only *half-truths*. And, *half-truths* are misleading lies. *Prosperity*

Theology is based upon a *half-truth* from the Scriptures. But the other half of its foundation is a *doctrine of demons* that suppresses and denies ample Scriptural evidence to the contrary.

Let's set one thing straight. God is not specifically opposed to his own children having or accumulating wealth, provided it is obtained by ethical and responsible means. Sure, there are many principles of the Bible that speak favorably about God's intentions to bless His own who live righteously. We shall be blessed in many different ways, some of which are tangible in the near-term present world and might include possessions and real estate. But there are numerous other Biblical principles that are intentionally sidestepped in order to make this errant teaching palatable and desirable as a "new" theology that tickles the ears of the hearers.

JESUS' EXAMPLE CONCERNING MONEY

Consider carefully Jesus as our role model for the philosophy of money. After leaving his family home in Nazareth, where he had worked with his hands in the building trades as a "marketplace minister" for decades, Jesus was essentially a migrating itinerant "minister" without a home for the final three years of His life. Jesus said that He had no regular place to lay His head at night (Matthew 8:20). He was a traveling prophet-teacher-healer, presumably staying in various homes along his journeys, such as with His friend Lazarus and his two sisters.

Jesus was not affluent, at least during this latter "ministry" phase of life, and did not advocate for the affluent. To the contrary, He said, *"Blessed are you who are poor, for yours is the kingdom of God. Blessed are you who hunger now, for you will be satisfied…But woe to you who are rich, for you have already received your comfort. Woe to you who are well fed now, for you will go hungry…Give to everyone who asks you, and if anyone takes what belongs to you, do not demand it back."* (Luke 6:20-21, 24-25, 30). It is recorded that on occasion He and His disciples lacked food. Perhaps you recall the miraculous feeding of the hungry multitudes with a handful of fish and loaves of bread or gathering cereal grains from a field on the Sabbath. Neither is the sign of an affluent man. Furthermore, He showed deference and great respect to John-the-baptizer, who very likely lived an extremely humble life without luxuries.

After gathering together the original apostles and disciples, His own mother and half-brothers thought Jesus had gone crazy. One may rationally speculate that Jesus' family came after Him out of shame and embarrassment over Jesus living like an itinerant prophet-teacher without returning home each night. *"When his family heard about this, they went to take charge of him, for they said 'He is out of his mind.'"* (Mark 3:21). That's not exactly the type of image some folks have about his mother Mary and his half-brothers. [Upon reflection, some Roman Catholics in particular might have a bit of trouble with that Scripture.]

King David prophetically spoke about Jesus in this predicament, *"I am a stranger to my brothers, an alien to my own mother's sons; for zeal for your house consumes me, and the insult of those who insult you fall on me."* (Psalm 69:8-9). This prophetic word was directly attributed to Jesus in the New Testament with the phrase, *"zeal for your house will consume me"*. (John 2:17). By the way, this was mentioned within the context of Jesus personally purging the Jewish Temple (intended for worship of Yahweh) of the moneychangers and salesmen of worship objects. Just like our present times, Jesus witnessed people personally prospering off of "church business" in His day, and He was disgusted by it. The zeal of the Spirit within Jesus could not tolerate the absurdity of people intentionally profiting financially from worship to the Creator. For opportunistic selfish gain they turned something sacred into something impure. It incensed the Spirit within Jesus and led to a harsh verbal and physical judgment.

Sometimes Jesus' basic financial needs were met by women who traveled with His contingent of disciples (Luke 8:1-3). Another time a need was met when a Greek Tetra-drachma silver coin was taken from a fish's mouth following a prophetic word of knowledge spoken by Jesus

(Matthew 17:27). These examples don't describe an affluent man.

When Jesus was living as a man on this planet, did He live like a wealthy king? Did the forerunner John-the-baptizer live like a wealthy king? Did any of the founding apostolic-prophetic leaders of the Church live like a wealthy king? Oh, please listen! Some well-intentioned Charismatics express at this time, *"I'm a child of the King, so I'm going to live like a prince (or princess)!"* It is hard to Biblically defend this concept of a *"nice God who is our 'buddy' and always prospers us with increased finances"* that is percolating through certain circles of contemporary Christian culture.

I'm not advocating monastic asceticism in the least, in which case someone beats his or her own body and lives in utter deprivation in an attempt to please God. But, I am asking that we accurately handle the written *logos* word of God in its entirety. We should at least make an honest effort to know the Scriptures and to grow in obeying them over time. That includes studying Biblical texts both *for* and *against* financial prosperity. That is something the proponents of *Prosperity Theology* avoid like the plague on this particular issue.

Did not Jesus say that it is better that a man voluntarily remove an offending body part that leads to sin than to retain it and suffer the consequences of idolatry and sin in hell? Note to self -- **hell is a real place of torment!** It is not at all difficult to prove this point by the Scriptures (see Revelation 20; Matthew 5:22, 29-30; Matthew 23:33; Matthew 25:41-46; Luke 16:19; 2 Peter 2:4). Scriptures *suggest* that even Jesus visited hell at the time of his crucifixion (1 Peter 3:19; Ephesians 4:9-10). I, too, have "seen" a subterranean hell in a spiritual dream/vision in which I was preaching to a demonic horde. Jesus' provocative (and likely hyperbolic) teaching about cutting off an offending body party to prevent entrance into hell indicates that we must be vigilant regarding the causes of sin, and in this case, to guard against the desire to obtain wealth. Since money and material possessions are bound to the source of greed, envy, oppression, and self-desire, then money and possessions can be a source of evil of great consequence. Friends, we take this too lightly in the West today. *"The* *love of money is a root of all kinds of evil."* (1 Timothy 6:10). Yet, so many of us worry ourselves silly to gain it at any cost.

Why can anyone who understands the reality of an eternal hell because of how he or she misused money have the audacity to cry out in ignorance, *"I'm a child of the King, so I'll live like a prince (or princess)!"* This isn't humility. This isn't altruistic. It is blatant boastful arrogance. Remember, hell is real! Hell is horrible, and it is forever! Jesus was not joking. If the love of money causes you to go to hell, was it worth it? *"What good is it for a man to gain the whole world, and yet lose or forfeit his very self?"* (Luke 9:25).

DEFINING "PROSPERITY" BIBLICALLY

There is wisdom in petitioning God to meet our <u>needs</u> in alignment with the Proverb revealed by Agur, *"...give me neither poverty nor riches, but give me only my daily bread. Otherwise, I may have too much and disown you and say 'Who is the Lord?' Or I may become poor and steal, and so dishonor the name of my God."* (Proverbs 30:8). He knew that having great wealth presents a tremendous challenge that few believers can handle. Righteously handling affluence takes wisdom and self-control; if not careful, one can become quickly ensnared by affluence.

One need only look at the disastrous results of rapidly obtained ill-gotten gains, such as from winning the lottery or from gambling. There is seldom a favorable long-term outcome for the recipient. Listen to these stern warnings: *"Such is the end of all who go after ill-gotten gain; it takes away the lives of those who get it."* (Proverbs 1:19). *"Ill-gotten treasures are of no value, but righteousness delivers from death."* (Proverbs 10:2). And, *"An inheritance quickly gained at the beginning will not be blessed at the end."* (Proverbs 20:21).

Consider the words of three founding Apostles regarding the connection between finances and faith. First, the Apostle James wrote with similarity to the words of Jesus in the Beatitudes (see Luke 6:20-36; Matthew 5:1-12), *"Listen, my dear brothers: Has not God chosen those who are <u>poor in the eyes of the world to be rich in faith</u> and to inherit the kingdom he promised those who love him? But you have insulted the poor. Is it not the rich who are exploiting you? Are they not the ones who are dragging you into court? Are they not the ones who are slandering the noble name of him to whom you belong?"* (James 2:5-7; emphasis added).

I, too, have noted the inverse proportionality between wealth and faith. Those who are financially poor are more naturally inclined to trust the Lord, and perhaps out of necessity. Was not the poor widow who gave her last two small copper coins into the offering commended by Jesus for her faith above those who had plenty to contribute? If you are looking for people of faith, don't look toward the wealthy in mansions, penthouses, and suburbia. You'll seldom observe any *risk-taking belief in action* with them, with the exception of when they are seeking to obtain wealth for themselves!

Second, the Apostle Peter emphasized that faith is *"of greater worth than gold"* (1 Peter 1:7). And third, the Apostle Paul wrote to the carnal Corinthian church that he was *"poor, yet making many rich; having nothing, and yet possessing everything."* (2 Corinthians 6:10; emphasis added). Paul described himself in financial terms similar to how Jesus described Himself. None of the three Apostles mentioned here focused their attention on money like today's *Prosperity Charlatans*. Rather, they focused on faith, as faith is the currency of the Kingdom of God.

However, God does bless the creation of honestly obtained wealth. *"Dishonest money dwindles away, but he who gathers money little by little makes it grow."* (Proverbs 13:11). But, many of the blessings God intends for obedient righteous living by His saved children are things that aren't measured by money or possessions. From a Kingdom of God perspective, the blessings of "prosperity" may be measured out to us in such ways as:

- The Fruit of the Spirit (see Galatians 5)

- The gifts of the Spirit (see 1 Corinthians 12 & 14; Ephesians 2 & 4)
- Close relationship with Jesus
- Influence among other people and nations
- A spouse
- Children (natural, adopted, and spiritual)
- Friends
- Health and longevity
- Wisdom and a sound mind
- Answered prayer
- Contentment and shalom (peace)

I remind myself often that the really valuable things in life are *Faith, Family, and Friends.* The Creator's blessings of prosperity are <u>not</u> measured *primarily* by wealth, although wealth can be one of the components of His blessings. If we judge by our natural eyes coupled to our greedy minds, we can be easily deceived. Many in the West live under the *illusion of blessing*, simply because they happen to live in affluence. But, it is a veneer! *"You say, 'I am rich; I have acquired wealth and do not need a thing.' But you do not realize that you are wretched, pitiful, poor, blind and naked. I counsel you to buy from me gold refined in the fire, so you can become rich; and white clothes to wear, so you can cover your shameful nakedness; and salve to put on your eyes so you can see. Those whom I love I rebuke and discipline. So be earnest, and repent."* (Revelation 3:17-19). The church of Laodicea in Revelation chapter 3 epitomizes our current Western worldview that elevates affluence. We are to obtain spiritual "gold refined by fire", meaning that which is virtuous and of eternal value. We are to obtain spiritual "white clothing", meaning that which is pure, forgiven, and redeemed by the Blood of the Lamb. And we are to apply spiritual "eye salve" so as to have the "eyes of our hearts" healed to correctly see the truth rather than deception or the *illusion of blessing*. It is my observation that few living in the West have this insight at present. Therefore, Revelation 3 says we need to be earnest and to repent. Our priorities must change!

However, I personally know many people who have a lot of wealth and possessions, including many who have millions of dollars. But, very few are living righteously in obedience to the Scriptures. They are very far from the Kingdom of God. We must not look with the *eyes of sight*, but rather with the *eyes of faith* from a Kingdom perspective. Financial blessings can easily turn into a snare for both the possessor of the materials (i.e., greed and worry over loss), as well as for the one who lacks the material possessions (i.e., envy, discontent, and bitterness). Both the rich and the poor can be easily driven by the demonic *spirit of poverty*. Financial prosperity has damaged the vision of billions of people over the millennia.

Few can handle the temptation of the idolatrous lure of wealth. Only those who have been tested in the little things and have been found faithful to the truth should be entrusted with more. Remember the parable of the Talents? Without wisdom, wealth is a deadly snare. One of the Church's early leaders, James, reinforced this principle saying that we lack because we ask with wrong motives, intending to fulfill our own lustful desires (see James 4:2-3). By His mercy the Creator restrains giving wealth to some of His followers for their own good. I repeat for emphasis, *"give me neither poverty nor riches"* (see Proverbs 30:8). We must learn to be content in all circumstances, either in plenty or in little. We must learn to discriminate between our *wants* and our *needs*. And, we must become generous and focused altruistically upon meeting others' needs before our own wants.

Friends, we just can't afford to select the Scriptures that we like and discard those we dislike. We can't choose only the pleasant ones. We need the *Whole Counsel of the LORD*, including those Scriptures that don't appeal to us. Without that objectivity, we're open to deception and serious errors. This is one area where many folks within the Church in the Third World have a greater appreciation of the Scriptures. They have endured greater hardships, such as economic and political uncertainty, denial of basic human "rights," and in some cases have faced fierce religious persecutions for standing up for the Gospel. The believers in the Church of the Third World have learned valuable lessons that seem to have been lost in the developed Western World over the decades since World War II. Consider the costs paid by the disciples of Jesus in China, Myanmar, Indonesia, Africa, and the Islamic states of the Middle East. Many believers have lost everything for their precious Savior Jesus! They have lost money, possessions, homes, family, and friends. They have endured imprisonment, torture, and beatings. And yet God is greatly *prospering* them in the midst of their financial poverty, lack, and material need!

Prosperity that comes from God should <u>not</u> be viewed mono-dimensionally as *prosperity = financial blessings.* Let's not be short sighted in understanding the breadth of the meaning of Biblical prosperity. Psalm 37 addresses the fact that many "wicked" people enjoy financial successes in life. They appear to be financially "blessed," and to some extent it is true. However, we must not envy those who do not operate from a Kingdom perspective toward wealth. Worldly standards of success and wealth are disturbing to God and should become disturbing to us as His followers (Luke 6:15). How much has the world's schematic been imprinted into our minds?

Those persecuted in other lands for the sake of the Gospel have much to say to the affluent Western "Church" today. Consider Hudson Taylor and Watchman Nee in China, William Carey in India, and the great intercessor Rees Howells of Wales, who were amply blessed with the Fruits of the Spirit and with many other spiritual blessings. Though they are physically dead, yet their testimonies still speak (see Hebrews 11:4). They lacked personal material possessions and paid the high price for the cause of Christ! Their priority was on knowing Jesus Christ, not on material possessions, as we are admonished, *"Set your minds on things above, not on earthly things."* (Colossians 3:2). *"Do not love the world or anything in the world. If anyone loves the world, the love of the Father is not in him. For everything in the world—the cravings of sinful man, the lust of his eyes and the boasting of what he has and does—comes not from the Father but from the world. The world and its desires pass away, but the man who does the will of God lives forever."* (1 John 2:15-17).

I've taken Path Clearer ministry teams to the historic sites in England and Wales where the Almighty forged and stretched the faith of William Carey, Hudson Taylor, Rees Howells, and Evan Roberts. We've prayed and lain prostrate on the floor while breathing in the carpet fibers in Moulton, England where Carey was a Particular Baptist preacher in the late 1700's. We've kneeled on the docks of Liverpool where Hudson Taylor spent the most difficult faith-building day of his entire life in 1853. On that day, Taylor departed alone from his dear sobbing mother to head to China as a missionary, fully depending on God's provision and protection. We've breathed the carpet fibers of the Bible College of Wales, where Rees Howells led private intercessory prayer to change events of world history during World War II. We've prayed inside of Moriah Chapel in Swansea, where the youthful Welsh Revival leader, Evan Roberts, pleaded with God in intercession a century ago, *"Bend me. Bend us."* These commendable British men-of-faith each paid a high price for his calling. Let us properly honor them and not belittle all other real soldiers-of-the-Cross with our contemporary flippant mind-numbing self-seeking *Prosperity Theology*.

Let's face the profound truth…__*Faith is the currency of the Kingdom of God; money is not!*__ Faith is defined as *risk-taking belief in action*. We can have plenty of money and yet have no faith. In that condition we will never be pleasing to God. We can even attend church regularly, read our Bibles diligently, and give regularly to the church or charities…and yet lack genuine faith.

The Way of the Cross of Christ is synonymous with the Baptism-by-Fire. We *must* undergo this Baptism-by-Fire as His obedient disciples. It will be extremely "expensive" for us, but not necessarily in monetary terms. The Cross of Christ can never be purchased by money. We must surrender, embrace the path of faith, and undergo death to self. This is the path of greatest challenge and greatest reward.

COMMON ERRORS OF *PROSPERITY THEOLOGY*

Brothers and sisters, there are things seriously wrong with *Prosperity Theology's* imbalanced over-emphasis on materialism and financial rewards. You can have loads of money and the appearance of prosperity, yet totally miss life-changing encounters with Jesus Christ. Jesus told us that it is extremely hard for a rich man to enter the Kingdom of Heaven (see Matthew 19:16-30). Sure, I desire for all of God's chosen to be blessed with abundant life, but genuine blessings from a Kingdom perspective are likely to look very different than the view espoused by the proponents of this "new" teaching. They strongly emphasize financial prosperity and neglect to be open toward plenty of other Scriptures running in the other direction. May we repent and, once again, agree with the great hymn of surrender (author is anonymous):

> *I have decided to follow Jesus.*
>
> *No turning back, no turning back.*
>
> *The cross before me; the world behind me.*
>
> *No turning back, no turning back.*
>
> *Though none go with me, still I will follow.*
>
> *No turning back, no turning back.*

What a shame if we're following Him just because we want Jesus to hand us a microphone, or a large bank account, or an annual ministry budget in the millions, or a Rolls Royce car, or a mansion on the lake, or a book contract, or our own television station. We need to follow Him simply because He is the Creator-Son and is inherently worthy of us doing so... not just to get some cookies from His hand. We need to shift our eyes from His hand to His face. After all, those who make it into eternity in His presence will forever declare that He is worthy of all praise. And everything that was carnal will have been burned up.

Have you not noticed that the proponents for this "new" teaching invariably are requesting money from *you* for the support of *his or her* agenda, which frequently includes lavish lifestyles and prominent ministries named after themselves? Think about it. Then think about it again. What's wrong with this picture? They often say to their audiences, *"You should invest a seed of faith into my ministry!"* If the principles they teach were entirely balanced and true, why not simply teach these principles freely with no expectation of receiving anything themselves? *Prosperity Theology* fills the pockets of its most effective proponents and cajolers. These effective salesmen receive the reward themselves for self-serving rhetoric and aberrant theology lessons. This type of theology "pays". It sometimes resembles a Ponzi scheme, a pyramid plan that keeps those at the top well fed and well dressed while the rank and file at the bottom must struggle to make a humble living in order to feed the beast above them. You might have heard of the phrase, "the greater fool".

However, in the Kingdom of God, this must not be spoken of you! A servant leader must not be greedy for money (see 1 Peter 5:2). In the *real* Kingdom of God, servanthood and generosity are the hallmarks of a mature disciple…not some so-called "leader" who pleads and begs for money on TV, radio, or from a pulpit. *He* cries and moans for your financial support for *his* ministry, and for *his* version of how to reach the world with *his* message, and for *his* own lavish lifestyle, and for *his* "dreams" about *his* kingdom on earth.

Rather, it is time that we hear other words like those of the prophet Ezekiel, *"Prophesy against the shepherds of Israel…'Woe to the shepherds of Israel who only take care of themselves! Should not shepherds take care of the flock…I am against the shepherds and will hold them accountable for my flock. I will remove them from tending the flock so that the shepherds can no longer feed themselves. I will rescue my flock from their mouths, and it will no longer be food for them.'"* (Ezekiel 34:2-12; emphasis added). And the prophet Zechariah also spoke of self-serving "shepherds" and declared this prophetic rebuke, *"This is what the LORD my God says: "Pasture the flock marked for slaughter. Their buyers slaughter them and go unpunished. Those who sell them say, 'Praise the LORD, I am rich!' Their own shepherds do not spare them."* ~~(Zechariah 11:4-5; emphasis added)~~. Note the attitude of the selfish shepherds who delight that they have made a profit off of their subordinated oppressed sheep. They just want to make a buck! They ultimately don't care for the welfare of their flock.

These selfish "shepherds" might present a pretty picture of an appealing "green tree of life" from the pulpit on stage. But behind the scenes, the followers who have paid with their offerings get the ol' switcheroo; they receive a lifeless brown tree that doesn't have a single green needle or leaf. The green tree is for the leader's benefit alone. He and his family will do just fine, thank you very much.

We have an abundance of self-seeking ravenous "shepherds" minding the flocks of today's local churches and so-called "Christian TV" audiences. According to the prophet Micah, they are no different than ancient Israel's money-seeking (false) prophets, priests, and kings, *"Her leaders judge for a bribe, her priests teach for a price, and her prophets tell fortunes for money..."* (Micah 3:11a). The spiritual leaders of Israel just wanted to make a buck!

It is time that the Church rises up and throws out its own filthy trash. If we don't, then the World will do it for us through critical documentaries, congressional hearings, and legal battles. If we followers of Jesus don't mind our own business, they'll make it their business to intervene, to oppose, to criticize, to scoff, and to mock. If we don't discern and judge this serious error correctly ourselves, the Lord will continue to judge the *Prosperity Charlatans* in the public arena using the Assyrians or Babylonians of the modern media. And, if we fail to correct these errant brothers and sisters, our own privileges as ministers of the Gospel might become more limited and damaged. *Prosperity Charlatans* are threatening the moral fiber of Judeo-Christian society and could bring serious damage to our own free expression and use of Biblical worldviews.

The line is being drawn <u>now</u> in the sand. Which side are you going to stand on? Are you going to side <u>with</u> the *Prosperity Charlatans* or <u>against</u>

them? What does the *Whole Counsel of the LORD* require of you?

Shouldn't judgment regarding *Prosperity Theology* <u>first</u> come from within the house of God? If we don't take care of this mess, then who will? Jesus warned us to meet our accuser before he or she takes us to court, to minimize or avert any further damage (Matthew 5:23-26). When we are in the wrong, we should meet the accuser half way. We should cut them off at the pass and bring the appropriate offerings of repentance with a humble and contrite spirit. The secular folks have good reason to be critical of *Prosperity Theology*. Shouldn't we, too, as followers of Jesus? Or are we just too gullible or self-absorbed to see the obvious?

Prosperity Theology is an appealing but dangerous rattlesnake. It has many close cousins – greed, theft, manipulation, self-seeking ambition, pretense, selfishness, elitism, and luxury. When we pick up a rattlesnake and stick it in our pocket, we shouldn't be surprised when we discover later that it has fangs and venom. We knew it was a rattlesnake when we first set our eyes upon it with desire. The trouble is that it looks good on the outside to those who earnestly desire wealth for themselves. But, love of the World puts us at enmity with the Creator.

Ask yourself, *"Do I control money? Or, does money control me?"* Money is a powerful "god" to many, if not most people. I've seen this ugly "god" up close and personal. Those who worship this "god" will go anywhere and do anything to obtain more of it. And sincerely religious people are not immune to this "god's" venom. Their words might suggest otherwise, but their actions will ring true to the "god" that they really serve.

Prosperity Theology is not Biblically balanced. It presents partial truths from selected Scriptures (which in themselves are true), while overlooking other compelling Scriptures that contradict it. It is an admixture of Biblical truths and demonic lies. Admixtures are powerful tools that are effective at deceiving others. The devil will put some honey into a bucketful of waste in order to get us to drink the poisonous solution. Admixtures are a common strategy of the devil.

The proponents of *Prosperity Theology* *"think that godliness is a means to financial gain."* (1 Timothy 6:5b). Paul continues in this passage regarding money to admonish disciples of Jesus to embrace sound theology and character,

> *"But godliness with contentment is great gain. For we brought nothing into the world, and we can take nothing out of it. But if we have food and clothing, we will be content with that. People who want to get rich fall into temptation and a trap and into many foolish and harmful desires that plunge men into ruin and destruction. For the love of money is a root of all kinds of evil. Some people, eager for money, have wandered from the faith and pierced themselves with many griefs. But you, man of God, flee from all this, and pursue righteousness, godliness, faith, love, endurance and gentleness. Fight the good fight of the faith. Take hold of the eternal life to which you were called when you made your good confession in the presence of many witnesses…Command those who are rich in this present world not to be arrogant nor to put their hope in wealth, which is so uncertain, but to put their hope in God, who richly provides us with everything for our enjoyment. Command them to do good, to be rich in good deeds, and to be generous and willing to share. In this way they will lay up treasure for themselves as a firm foundation for the coming age, so that they may take hold of the life that is truly life."* (1 Timothy 6:6-12, 17-19).

We should be prudent to give our financial contributions only to those ministries and local churches that are genuinely honoring to God. Identify those serving His Kingdom's purposes on earth efficiently, selflessly and without waste. Have you not seen reports of leaders of the prosperity movement who live in grandiose multi-million dollar estates? To add insult to injury, some ironically and deceptively term their mansions as pastors' "parsonages" to benefit from tax-exempt status. They pay themselves massive salaries as so-called "pastors," with some earning $500,000+ per year in salary — all the while exploiting the generosity of those who live on meager wages. Their lifestyles resemble those of the *Rich-and-Famous*. They are celebrities to be adored. Shame on anyone who continues to feed this beast! Cut off his or her food supply!

These wealthy televangelists and other so-called "ministers of the Gospel" (which is an overt misnomer) forcefully argue to their critics, *"But our financial books are audited by outside accounting firms. That means we have high ethical standards."* Oh, this is a cheap magician's trick! It is a simple slight-of-hand to keep your attention off of some really important questions. An *audit* does not mean that you solicit, receive, and spend the donated money righteously or ethically! It only means that you allocated the monies into the appropriate categories in your accounting software spreadsheets and general ledger so that it passes muster with the auditing firm and the IRS. That's all that an external audit does.

They can pay their family members hundreds of thousands of dollars as *pseudo-employees*, provided they allocate it into the correct accounting column. They can pay enormous amounts for "Presidential Suites" in posh 5-Star hotels at resorts while on ministry events (i.e., "vacations"), provided they allocate it into the correct accounting column. They can live in multi-million dollar mansions themselves as "parsonages," provided they allocate it to the correct accounting column. And they can also "give" to their own children as *pseudo-employees* expensive homes as so-called "parsonages" for their perceived assistance to the ministry, provided they allocate it to the correct accounting column. Completing an audit does not mean that someone is handling money righteously or wisely! It just means they've put it in the appropriate categories as per the standards of acceptable accounting policies. Don't be deceived.

Do you get the point? If it looks like manure, feels like manure, and smells like manure, you can bet it is manure! Who cares how they allocate it in the audit report? It is a stinking mess. And there are plenty of these *Prosperity Charlatans* operating on TV and radio — and many of their "cousins" serve as pastors in many churches every day in the West. On a typical day's worth of so-called "Christian" TV programming, we can see

—

a dozen of these prosperity-centric programs. Sadly, they are also rapidly infusing this error into the Third World via satellite TV and expensive foreign ministry trips. The sickness is rapidly spreading around the globe.

These greedy excesses are not unfamiliar to students of Church history. The Roman Catholic Church and its Orthodox kinfolk did the same ever since the Dark Ages. They milked the poor to build religious kingdoms of men, to gather gold and silver for ornate cathedrals and whitewashed marble tombs, and to give the appearance of glory to man-made institutions. The former greedy Roman Catholic leaders also sold indulgences for the presumed forgiveness of sins, thus granting man-made assurances of eternal consequences. Martin Luther made some correct observations about those issues during the Reformation. It seems that bilking money out of followers is an ancient art of Christendom.

But the Catholics no longer have a corner on this practice. Today the greedy Protestant *Prosperity Charlatans* "sell" their donors on the *quid pro quo* principle! They declare if you give a "seed" to *them*, then you'll reap a fruitful reward from *God*. It imputes an anticipated return-on-investment (ROI). Sometimes they even declare brazenly it will be 30-fold, 60-fold, or 100-fold. The *Prosperity Charlatans* say things like, *"The Lord told me to tell you personally, 'Give to this ministry $1,000 right now! Go ahead and give us your offering by check, cash, or credit card. Put your faith behind it, as the Lord told me to tell you that you'll get a 30-fold blessing back for this seed sown today. Amen?'"* Ironically, you are asked or manipulated to give to the preacher-man's ministry — and somehow God will give back to you as the donor. The preacher-man receives the benefit without the responsibility for fulfilling the ROI obligations. You just selfishly fill in the blank of whatever you're wishing for! The modern day Protestant preacher-man says, *"You scratch my back, and God will scratch yours."* And, to keep you a happy donor, they'll send you a token prayer cloth, or a prayer guide on a business card, or another cheap gimmick gift. In many cases that cheap gift is your return-on-investment!

But Jesus said in John 15:7 that we're entitled to ask of Him in accordance with the principles of *remaining in Him* and *His word remaining within us.* He isn't just a Jesus-the-Santa-man or Jesus-the-Genie-man who grants our every fond desire. There are conditions, and it requires a relationship of knowing His *logos* written Word and the Holy Spirit's *rhema* revelation Word. That close relationship gives to us revelation of His desires, and His desires are the ones that He then fulfills.

It should be noted that the principles of *return-on-investment* for the *seed-of-faith* sown each have a legitimate Biblical basis. It can be supported by Scripture, but only as principles. However, they are not assured specific promises for a specific circumstance. Often the anticipated rewards are not realized by the "seed" donors. They think unwisely in advance, *"I'll give this seed to the man-of-God, and I expect to receive that reward from God."* This can be a disheartening reality. Giving for the motivation of receiving direct financial blessings can produce disappointments, because it is built on a faulty foundation. Biblical *principles* are not *guarantees* of a particular outcome for an individual in a particular circumstance. They are *general* patterns, not *specific* assurances or insurance policies. This errant thinking can and does destroy hope, because the hope was in the wrong person, place, or thing.

Another disgraceful and self-serving notion expressed by the proponents of *Prosperity Theology* is a rationale that, *"If you preach it, you must live it."* To the proponents it means one must be unashamedly decorated with tangible evidence of financial wealth for all to see. You're supposed to flaunt it, like the pretentious gold "bling" necklaces on a street rapper in the ghetto. I've heard them say, *"You're a child of the King, so live like a prince (or princess)!"* I've heard them say, *"If I don't drive a luxury car, then the sheep that I pastor will doubt whether this 'seed' principle works."* This notion is ridiculous and is indefensible by anything more than a cursory imbalanced look at the Bible. This emphasis on personal wealth is about the pride and pretentious image of the minister and is a convenient marketing device to generate additional funds. It's ultimately idolatry of money that stems from lusts of the flesh. Jesus is always more concerned with the heart, rather than the image.

These *Prosperity Charlatans* are preaching an aberrant version of the Gospel for personal profit. Paul admonished the Corinthian believers, *"Unlike so many, we do not peddle the word of God for profit. On the contrary, in Christ we speak before God with sincerity, like men sent from God."* (see 2 Corinthians 2:17; emphasis added). The Apostle Paul said it was common even back in the early days of the Church for many ministers to be money-sucking leeches with false messages and false motives. In contrast he characterized his own ministry with these poignant words, *"sorrowful, yet always rejoicing; poor, yet making many rich; having nothing, and yet possessing everything."* (2 Corinthians 6:10; emphasis added).

We have a saying in the Deep South about things that aren't true – *That dog don't hunt!* In this context the advance of the genuine Gospel is accompanied by hardship, persecution, rejection, and financial difficulties. So, relative to Paul's candid and humble example the self-serving *show-me-the-money* messages of the *Prosperity Charlatans* stir up a strong word within my Spirit - *That dog don't hunt!*

This aberrant theology also fosters and feeds *idolatry* within the folks who *worship* the so-called *man-of-God* (or *woman-of-God*). The simple-minded devout followers adore these wealthy televangelists and mega-church pastors, while the latter have their pockets lined with cash and have their "cathedrals" erected on large campuses. The idolatrous followers envy the leader's anointing and abandon all discernment at the door. Thus, the followers of *Prosperity Charlatans* elevate the preacher-man to an *idol* and are so enamored with the *man-of-God* that they defend the preacher-man with blind loyalty, regardless of the truth. Examples of this idolatry of prosperity gospel proponents were clearly shown to me in spiritual dreams, indicating that the idolatry distorts the eyesight of the followers and takes them captive to their own desires. I later literally saw those prophetic dreams realized before my very eyes while traveling in Africa and Eastern Europe. There are millions of people who adore and idolize these preacher-man ministers as "gods." I am not exaggerating! I have witnessed it many times over.

The loyal followers of the *Prosperity Charlatans* think erroneously, *"Oh…look how the Lord has blessed the man-of-God!"* But I say to you -- God has not blessed that man! The preacher-man has merely ripped you off, and you paid for it while smiling. Quit feeding this ravenous beast that is stealing from the Kingdom of God for his or her own agenda. Babylon, the sinister financial system of the World, is alive and well in many churches and ministries. Not only are those men and women holding the microphone guilty, but so are the loyal followers participating in the pews and watching broadcasts at home from the comfort of their Lazyboy recliners.

Oh, where are the modern Saint George-the-dragon-slayers, who will courageously attack this beast of *Prosperity Theology* precisely and accurately using the logos and rhema Word of God? Where are the genuine prophets today? Or, are too many of them so compromised by embracing this lucrative erroneous theology that they can't speak out against it with any level of authority?

What about frugality and responsibility toward the donors and God? In many cases the monies solicited by prosperity preachers are used inefficiently. Do we really need gold-leaf throne chairs for the "royalty" and guests on these so-called "Christian" TV broadcast sets? Do we even need their type of so-called "Christian" TV and radio broadcasts? Do we need any more $20 Million "cathedrals," when each of our bodies is the temple of the Holy Spirit? Do we need to spend another $2 Million on a so-called "crusade" that lasts only a few days in Asia or Africa? For that price tag the "crusade" will have high visibility on satellite TV, extravagant decorations, rows of white cloth-covered chairs for politicians and dignitaries on or near the illuminated stage, a huge choir, blocks of lavish hotel rooms, and a top-dollar advertising budget. The walls and businesses on the streets nearby will be emblazoned with thousands of posters with the famous preacher-man's smiling face.

I wonder if some of these "crusade" events are being done largely for the sake of the TV viewing audience back home in the States or Europe. This sure seems like expensive advertising to solicit even more funds from donors back home, yet coincidentally at the same time giving the impression of "changing the world for Jesus". How much of it is real? How much of it is marketing and the *illusion-of-blessing*? It must grieve the Holy Spirit to see the waste of money thrown around by some of these top-tier ministries. At least the Spirit within me is deeply grieved by their excesses and showmanship, and I've been there overseas and have seen it with my own eyes. Been there, seen that!

The *Prosperity Charlatans* plead with their followers, *"It is so expensive to host 'crusades' and television ministry events. We simply can't survive unless you help us meet this month's financial obligations!"* Don't be fooled for a moment; similar or higher value long-term impact for the Kingdom of God can be obtained for perhaps one tenth (or less) of that amount by other honorable ministry leaders. A tremendous amount can be accomplished by anointed disciples with integrity who are poor in resources yet are rich in faith and discipline! I know this first hand from many experiences overseas in Asia, Africa, Europe, and the UK. A small amount of money can accomplish great things if it is the hands of trustworthy men-and women-of-God.

CONCLUSION OF THE MATTER

Brothers and Sisters, please heed this warning. This "new" aberrant theology (often associated with pentecostals and charismatics) is not restricted to the USA. It is permeating the Church around the globe and to the detriment of our overseas brothers and sisters. Many Christians around the globe are dismayed and perplexed by the over-emphasis of *Prosperity Theology*. Honestly, they don't need it in their land. We don't need it here, and they don't need it over there. To me it resembles exporting cigarettes for profit into the markets of foreign countries. It should stop. Period. We're exporting garbage over the airwaves during many of these "Christian" TV and radio programs — because the preacher-man has enough money to purchase airtime.

Some Christians will find these words highly provocative and unsettling. Good! But please don't misunderstand, I'm not *"throwing the baby out with the bathwater."* I am attempting to bring about a long-overdue correction in view of an over-emphasis that has produced a faulty theological foundation. The correction seeks to address the need for a balanced view of the message of prosperity and to *also* embrace the difficulties, challenges, and chastisements from the hand of the Lord. If you doubt this advice, go spend some time with the "Persecuted Believers" in a land that is hostile toward the Gospel.

In summary, some of the significant problems manifested by *Prosperity Theology* include:

(1) It promotes a selfish spirit of greed and manipulation by the soliciting ministry for its own benefits;

(2) It instills a *quid pro quo* expectation that God will perform a reward for the donor, and it elevates greed within the donor;

(3) It results in poor accountability and responsibility regarding how to spend the funds received wisely, righteously, efficiently, and effectively;

(4) It denies or suppresses an abundance of contrary "opposing" Scriptures about the value of difficulty, hard work, suffering, and discipline in life; and

(5) It lacks universal applicability, such as amongst the poor of the Third World.

Finally, may we always be generous to give to the Kingdom of God and for the furtherance of the Gospel of Jesus Christ (see 2 Corinthians

---

8 & 9). It is not my intention to turn off the tap of the giving hydrant. Rather, it is to refocus giving in order to avoid giving any money to *Prosperity Charlatans* or to ineffective or inefficient ministries. It is more important that we give to Judeo-Christian organizations and churches that are efficient conduits of the genuine Kingdom of God than to selfish "shepherds" who are the personal beneficiaries of the largesse of donors. Please seek out ministries led by servant leaders of integrity and hold them accountable. And, speaking of selfish shepherds…

2

Dam Ministries

"Be shepherds of God's flock that is under your care, serving as overseers — not because you must, but because you are willing as God wants you to be; not greedy for money, but eager to serve; not lording it over those entrusted to you, but being examples to the flock." (1 Peter 5:2-3)

I firmly believe that the Holy Spirit wants no dam ministries and no dam ministers!

Before I elaborate on this remark, let me first paint a picture for you. A rainbow trout darts around gleefully...if a fish can be happy...as it moves downstream experiencing the pleasures of a cool country stream. The water passes over smooth rocks as it flows along its effortless gravitational stroll. The stream careens left and then right through fields from which dissolved minerals and nutrients are leached from the soil. Life-sustaining oxygen is absorbed from the air by the churning at the surface. All is well with the world surrounding this happy little trout.

However, abruptly the stream's natural flow is slowed to a crawl as it reaches the entrance to a large body of water. On the bright side, there is more space to roam about freely in search of the next meal and many other fish to meet. But something is wrong, gravely wrong!

Without any control over his own destiny as a freshwater trout, the fish's freedom has been suspended. The life-giving stream in which he was journeying emptied into a man-made pond. All because of a dam!

Without this dam, he would be free to continue his journey. Like a bad movie, this dam redefines "life" as he now would come to know it. This place no longer remotely resembles a flowing stream of crystal clear water. Sure, it has plenty of volume and other fish. But it has accumulated toxins and debris as the water at the surface gradually evaporated. There are discarded plastic bags, old rubber tires, and rusty soda cans. This dam held back the potential of life to flow freely downstream. It held back the innumerable possibilities for this little fish.

LET THE RIVER FLOW

Many local churches are nothing more than dammed ponds. The pastors or leaders think that because they founded it or were hired to run it that all of the people therein are "their" possessions by divine entitlement. These pastors hoard "their" fish that have accumulated in "their" congregations by building a dam to stop them from moving on in their spiritual gifts and callings in life. These leaders even stop them from leaving their control. These pastors judge their success by the number of fish and the size of the pond blocked by their own dams.

We need to burst these man-made dams and let the river flow freely! In the Scriptures, the Spirit of God is sometimes referred to as like a "river". He flows wherever He desires. Just as the wind flows, so does the Spirit's river. A river (or wind for that matter) stops flowing wherever resistance is encountered. Resistance to the Spirit's river has a quenching and stifling effect.

The prophet Ezekiel has a vision or spiritual journey led by a Heaven-sent "man" (i.e., interpreted as an angel). In it the prophet makes the following observations concerning a river of water flowing from under the Temple mount in Jerusalem:

> *The man brought me back to the entrance of the temple, and I saw*
> *water coming out from under the threshold of the temple toward the*

east (for the temple faced east). The water was coming down from under the south side of the temple, south of the altar. He then brought me out through the north gate and led me around the outside to the outer gate facing east, and the water was flowing from the south side. As the man went eastward with a measuring line in his hand, he measured off a thousand cubits and then led me through water that was ankle-deep. He measured off another thousand cubits and led me through water that was knee-deep. He measured off another thousand and led me through water that was up to the waist. He measured off another thousand, but now it was a river that I could not cross, because the water had risen and was deep enough to swim in—a river that no one could cross. He asked me, "Son of man, do you see this?" Then he led me back to the bank of the river. When I arrived there, I saw a great number of trees on each side of the river. He said to me, "This water flows toward the eastern region and goes down into the Arabah, where it enters the Sea. When it empties into the Sea, the water there becomes fresh. Swarms of living creatures will live wherever the river flows. There will be large numbers of fish, because this water flows there and makes the salt water fresh; so where the river flows everything will live. Fishermen will stand along the shore; from En Gedi to En Eglaim there will be places for spreading nets. The fish will be of many kinds—like the fish of the Great Sea. But the swamps and marshes will not become fresh; they will be left for salt. Fruit trees of all kinds will grow on both banks of the river. Their leaves will not wither, nor will their fruit fail. Every month they will bear, because the water from the sanctuary flows to them. Their fruit will serve for food and their leaves for healing." (Ezekiel 47:1-12; emphasis added).

There are many key insights to be gleaned from this angelic encounter. As the river flowed out of the Temple mount eastward, the waters progressively increased in depth. This might be due to the coalescence of shallow waters dispersed over a larger area into a narrower river channel of greater depth further downstream. Wherever the waters were flowing its effect was lifegiving! This is clearly emphasized with regard to the numerous fish that attracted fishermen to the banks of the river, as well as to various kinds of fruit-bearing trees along the river's shoreline. The river gave life to everything it encountered.

This passage speaks symbolically to the attraction of a diversity of peoples to the "river," the latter of which represents the flow of the Holy Spirit. The prophet Isaiah recorded, *"...my house will be called a house of prayer for all nations."* (Isaiah 56:7b; emphasis added). Seven centuries later Jesus recited this same passage upon His "Triumphal Entry" into Jerusalem, and this remark was expressed while within the Temple (see Mark 11:17 and Matthew 21:13). Furthermore, Isaiah also recorded, *"And I... am about to come and gather all nations and tongues, and they will come and see my glory."* (Isaiah 66:18; emphasis added). The key point is simply this -- wherever the waters of the Holy Spirit are flowing, that is where life is happening! The emphasis is upon *flowing* water, not upon *stagnant* water (compare verses 9 and 11). Stagnant water occurs whenever the flow is stopped by a dam.

That being said, why do we tolerate dam ministers or dam ministries? The book of Ephesians instructs the *five-fold* leaders of the Church to equip others for the service of ministry. All disciples of Jesus are to be ministers of the Gospel, not just the founding pastor, or the senior pastor, or the bishop, or whatever leadership title they desire to use.

Some of the dam ministers parade around like alpha male apes elevating their image using an *honorary* doctorate for a title of respect. This is driven by pride and in some cases insecurity. They refer to themselves as "Doctor so and so", even though they did not *earn* the title by diligent academic study and work. They did not work for that honor; it was just given to them as a "freebee". At the least, this is a misleading exaggeration. Check the resumes and credentials of ministers who use the title of "Doctor". I've seen charlatans using honorary doctorates to broadcast a pretentious image that is not deserved.

Spiritual leaders need to learn to be servants who practice *catch-and-release* fishing. There are many styles of fishing: dragnets, seines, rods and reels, multi-hook jigs, among others. Most of the time we go fishing for keeps. We intend to eat the fish that we catch. But, some of the most talented sports fishermen practice catch-and-release methods. The goal isn't to keep the fish. It is just to catch the fish for a brief moment, assess its size and stage of development, and then send it on its way.

Wouldn't it be wonderful if pastors and other ministry leaders viewed believers and the potential members for "their" congregations from this perspective? Why not try holding people lightly within an open palm, rather than a clinched fist? Believers and disciples aren't the personal possession of those doing the teaching and training! We don't own anyone, and we don't have the right to subject them to our control. The disciples should willingly follow a mature spiritual leader, but not due to the leader's control over them. If leaders would just catch them for a while and impart teaching, correction, and training, and then release them to go on their way, wouldn't we have a much healthier Church? Everyone would live knowing that they were "free" to move on down the stream as the Lord leads them in new directions with new opportunities.

Send in the dam busters! Remove the branches and debris built up by the beavers. Let us esteem the *catch-and-release* ministers of the Gospel of Jesus! Be a conduit and not a pond. Send in the servant-leaders who don't lord it over others. Servant-leaders get underneath those in need and lift them up (see Matthew 20:25-28). Jesus himself came to serve, not to be served! Greatness is measured by serving from below, not lording it over from above.

WHERE ARE THE GOOD SHEPHERDS?

As a parallel metaphor there are serious warnings in Ezekiel chapter 34 to "shepherds" who use the flock of "sheep" for their own personal gain.

Both shepherds and sheep should heed these warnings:

> *The word of the LORD came to me: "Son of man, prophesy against the shepherds of Israel; prophesy and say to them: 'This is what the Sovereign LORD says:* <u>*Woe to the shepherds of Israel who only take care of themselves! Should not shepherds take care of the flock? You eat the curds, clothe yourselves with the wool and slaughter the choice animals, but you do not take care of the flock. You have not strengthened the weak or healed the sick or bound up the injured. You have not brought back the strays or searched for the lost. You have ruled them harshly and brutally.*</u> *So they were scattered because there was no shepherd, and when they were scattered they became food for all the wild animals. My sheep wandered over all the mountains and on every high hill. They were scattered over the whole earth, and no one searched or looked for them." 'Therefore, you shepherds, hear the word of the LORD: As surely as I live, declares the Sovereign LORD, because my flock lacks a shepherd and so has been plundered and has become food for all the wild animals, and because my shepherds did not search for my flock but cared for themselves rather than for my flock, therefore, O shepherds, hear the word of the LORD: This is what the Sovereign LORD says:* <u>*I am against the shepherds and will hold them accountable for my flock. I will remove them from tending the flock so that the shepherds can no longer feed themselves. I will rescue my flock from their mouths, and it will no longer be food for them.*</u> *" 'For this is what the Sovereign LORD says: I myself will search for my sheep and look after them. As a shepherd looks after his scattered flock when he is with them, so will I look after my sheep. I will rescue them from all the places where they were scattered on a day of clouds and darkness. I will bring them out from the nations and gather them from the countries, and I will bring them into their own land. I will pasture them on the mountains of Israel, in the ravines and in all the settlements in the land. I will tend them in a good pasture, and the mountain heights of Israel will be their grazing land. There they will lie down in good grazing land, and there they will*

feed in a rich pasture on the mountains of Israel. I myself will tend my sheep and have them lie down, declares the Sovereign LORD. I will search for the lost and bring back the strays. I will bind up the injured and strengthen the weak, but the sleek and the strong I will destroy. I will shepherd the flock with justice. " 'As for you, my flock, this is what the Sovereign LORD says: I will judge between one sheep and another, and between rams and goats. Is it not enough for you to feed on the good pasture? Must you also trample the rest of your pasture with your feet? Is it not enough for you to drink clear water? Must you also muddy the rest with your feet? Must my flock feed on what you have trampled and drink what you have muddied with your feet? " 'Therefore this is what the Sovereign LORD says to them: See, I myself will judge between the fat sheep and the lean sheep. Because you shove with flank and shoulder, butting all the weak sheep with your horns until you have driven them away, I will save my flock, and they will no longer be plundered. I will judge between one sheep and another. <u>*I will place over them one shepherd, my servant David, and he will tend them; he will tend them and be their shepherd. I the LORD will be their God, and my servant David will be prince among them. I the LORD have spoken.*</u> *" 'I will make a covenant of peace with them and rid the land of wild beasts so that they may live in the desert and sleep in the forests in safety. I will bless them and the places surrounding my hill. I will send down showers in season; there will be showers of blessing. The trees of the field will yield their fruit and the ground will yield its crops; the people will be secure in their land. They will know that I am the LORD, when I break the bars of their yoke and rescue them from the hands of those who enslaved them. They will no longer be plundered by the nations, nor will wild animals devour them. They will live in safety, and no one will make them afraid. I will provide for them a land renowned for its crops, and they will no longer be victims of famine in the land or bear the scorn of the nations. Then they will know that I, the LORD their God, am with them and that they, the house of Israel, are my people, declares the Sovereign LORD. You my sheep, the sheep of my pasture, are people, and I am your God, declares the Sovereign LORD.'" (Ezekiel 34:1-31; emphasis added).*

This passage penned by the prophet Ezekiel around the time of the Babylonian captivity indicates that Yahweh is fiercely opposed to shepherds who only look after their own self-interests. Similar warnings are reiterated in Zechariah chapter 11. God will judge selfish shepherds. His plan (as per Ezekiel 34:23-24) was that the Messiah of the lineage of King David (i.e., interpreted as Jesus of Nazareth) would be a benevolent selfless shepherd. That was to take effect in approximately five centuries after this prophetic word was declared.

Likewise, shepherds today should be reminded that the True Church belongs to Jesus and the sheep thereof belong to Him. The sheep were purchased by His blood on the Cross. They were not purchased by any pastor, minister, or congregation. Therefore, the sheep are not the personal possessions of any pastor, minister, or congregation! How often do we recognize the error in local churches whenever the leaders assert that this is "their" ministry and the followers are part of "their" congregation. The followers are not possessions. The sheep are not owned by any local church, even if that congregation is where they have chosen to hang their hats for a season of life. The sheep all belong to God.

The Gospel of Matthew reports that, *"Jesus went through all the towns and villages, teaching in their synagogues, preaching the good news of the kingdom and healing every disease and sickness. When he saw the crowds, he had compassion on them, because they were harassed and helpless, like sheep without a shepherd."* (Matthew 9:35-36; emphasis added). Just as the Hebrew prophet Ezekiel recorded, Jesus too saw this same problem. But Jesus came as the fulfillment of Ezekiel's prediction. Jesus is the "Good Shepherd". He is very concerned about the condition of people. Leaders of churches and ministries should aspire to follow Jesus' example; they should strive to be good shepherds and to give sacrificially of themselves to meet the needs of the flock. Leaders should also heed the words of wisdom of Edgar Guest in his poem entitled, *Sermons We See*:

I'd rather see a sermon than hear one any day;

I'd rather one should walk with me than merely tell the way.

The eye's a better pupil and more willing than the ear,

Fine counsel is confusing, but example's always clear;

And the best of all the preachers are the men who live their creeds,

For to see good put in action is what everybody needs.

I soon can learn to do it if you'll let me see it done;

I can watch your hands in action, but your tongue too fast may run.

And the lecture you deliver may be very wise and true,

But I'd rather get my lessons by observing what you do;

For I might misunderstand you and the high advice you give,

But there's no misunderstanding how you act and how you live.

When I see a deed of kindness, I am eager to be kind.

When a weaker brother stumbles and a strong man stays behind

Just to see if he can help him, then the wish grows strong in me

To become as big and thoughtful as I know that friend to be.

And all travelers can witness that the best of guides today

Is not the one who tells them, but the one who shows the way.

One good man teaches many, men believe what they behold;

One deed of kindness noticed is worth forty that are told.

Who stands with men of honor learns to hold his honor dear,

For right living speaks a language which to everyone is clear.

Though an able speaker charms me with his eloquence, I say,

I'd rather see a sermon than to hear one, any day.

UNDER A LEADER'S AUTHORITY OR UNDER A LEADER'S THUMB

We are clearly instructed in the Word to be subject to our leaders, whether they are spiritual leaders, governmental leaders, or leaders within our family. I don't intend to belabor the point in favor of authorities here, as it has been effectively addressed by many Christian authors and is well supported by many Scriptures (e.g., Romans 13:1-6; Titus 3:1; 1 Peter 2:13-25; Matthew 22:21; Matthew 23:1-8; and 1 Tim 2:1-2). Many people in the Western World have a strong sense of independence, and it often stretches into outright rebellion and/or anarchy. Therefore, we need to hear Scripture's clear admonishments concerning voluntary subjection to authorities. We need to demonstrate *willingness to yield* and *to be persuadable* by someone in authority. We need to have teachable spirits and be in relationships of accountability and authority. This is for our own personal good, as well as for the protection of our families and society in general.

However, that is not to say that one is to <u>never</u> challenge, disregard, or disobey an authority's counsel in one's life. From the Scriptures and various personal experiences as a leader (and as a follower of other leaders), I firmly believe that one is, in fact, obligated to challenge, disregard, or disobey the counsel of an authority in certain cases involving misconduct by the leader. Several of the principle reasons are considered below.

Sometimes leaders with positional authority are in overt rebellion and sin against God. They can use their positions of influence to mislead, to abuse, to control, and/or to manipulate others (e.g., this is consistent with the spirit of witchcraft). To follow their aberrant counsel is not wise.

By way of example, David preserved his own life by leaving King Saul. However, David would not go so far as to be on the offensive to attack "God's anointed." David worked patiently within the system, but eventually he armed himself for self-preservation and left the King's presence. This was a necessary defensive action by David. This demonstrates that defensive action to preserve one's life and integrity was appropriate, but offensive vengeance was not. This principle should guide our conduct when we are forced to take action against an authority operating in error.

When we perceive that a leader is overtly wrong in a serious matter, we should appeal to the leader/authority as the first course using truth-in-love. We should seek to clarify if either we are in error or whether he/she is in error, or alternatively both of us are in error. According to the words of Jesus, one might then need to broaden the sphere of folks involved in confronting the errant leader – *"If your brother sins against you, go and show him his fault, just between the two of you. If he listens to you, you have won your brother over. But if he will not listen, take one or two others along, so that 'every matter may be established by the testimony of two or three witnesses.' If he refuses to listen to them, tell it to the church; and if he refuses to listen even to the church, treat him as you would a pagan or a tax collector."* (Matthew 18:15-17). Note that Jesus instructs that we should have nothing to do with a man such as this! Jesus is saying in this case that separation is the right thing to do. Hopefully, one or both of the parties will yield to God's counsel. If not, then one must move to the next level, which is to take a subsequent action step (e.g., to leave).

There are ample evidences of spiritual leaders in both the Old Testament and the New Testament where they appealed to or directly confronted error in other leaders who have some spiritual or governmental authority. Here's a short list of ten examples:

- Moses confronted Pharoah

- Nathan confronted King David

- Elijah confronted King Ahab and Queen Jezebel

- Elijah confronted 850 false prophets of Baal and Asherah

- Michaiah confronted King Ahab

- Jeremiah confronted King Jehoiakim

- Jeremiah confronted the false prophet Hananiah

- Jesus confronted the Pharisees and Sadducees, who had spiritual authority

- Jesus confronted the Herodians, who had territorial authority

- Paul confronted Peter for "Judaising" Gentile believers

Confrontation is often necessary! One especially profound example of confrontation within the nascent Church era is Peter and his colleagues confronting the High Priest and the Sanhedrin (consisting of the full assembly of the elders of Israel) in Acts chapter five. The religious authorities were forcefully attacking and oppressing the leaders of this new movement. But Peter passionately exclaimed with boldness, *"We must obey God rather than men!"* (Acts 5:29b). This is overt defiance of religious authority! No question whatsoever! But the religious authorities were in gross misconduct in persecuting Jesus' disciples and demanding them to stop obeying what Jesus had commanded them to do. The spiritual leaders of the Sanhedrin had authority, but they were in overt sin, and Peter declared that he would not obey their errant counsel.

The point I am addressing has to do with whenever an authority *requires* someone to disobey the Lord's written Word or the Spirit's leading. In these cases we should first make an appeal to the leader verbally or in writing. Then, if the outcome is not successful, we are at liberty to take additional actions. For instance, we could draw other individuals into the confrontation with the authority (e.g., see Matthew 18:15-17), or disregard their counsel, or choose to separate from their imposed authority.

It should be noted that spiritual authorities are granted permission *voluntarily* to exercise authority over our lives. That permission may be rescinded voluntarily, and at certain times it would be most prudent to do so. [However, in general this is not the case for submission of children to parents or for citizens toward governmental authorities.]

The issue of authority is very important to our well-being. But it must also be balanced with regard to other essential truths. Authority can be abusive. Haven't you heard about cases of child molesters who have authority in local churches? Or how about heavy-handed shepherds who manipulate individuals and won't permit people to make personal decisions? Or how about ministry leaders who thrive on *power-over-people* that is empowered by the demonic spirits of religion and pride, like modern day Pharisees? Or how about ministry leaders who "use" the system to their own personal financial gain in order to build their own kingdom, while milking those who support their appetites? In these cases, we should not just *"turn the other cheek"* and take whatever they dish out at us.

Furthermore, as a leader with a prophetic gifting and calling, I am often challenged by the Lord to hear, to see, and to discern…and then subsequently to confront, to challenge, and to uproot error. It comes with the territory. My perspective on authority is also tempered by first hand experience of abuse of authority within church leadership. There are appropriate times when one should challenge the authority of a ministry leader.

In his practical, timely, and relevant book entitled *Surviving the Anointing*, David Ravenhill wrote about the differences in a spiritual leader who is either a genuine benevolent "father" or a dictatorial "Pharaoh" (2007, pages 126-128). Pharaohs exercise overt power, control, manipulation, enslavement, restraint, and punishment, among other oppressive behaviors. Brothers and sisters, we need to support genuine "fathers" of the faith, those leaders who support us from below, not lord it over us from above. I believe we should challenge and confront "Pharaohs" and not support them with our time, talent, or funds.

Authority can be misused, and when it is, it becomes abusive. When it is abusive, it should be confronted. And, when necessary people who have been *under the thumb of a leader* should "vote with their feet."

BODIES, BUILDINGS, AND BUDGETS

These days doesn't it seem to all come down to numbers? Numbers, numbers, everywhere!

"Pastor, how many are you runnin' these days?"

"How many seats have you been fillin' up?"

"How many acres of land have you purchased?"

"How much you bringin' in these days?"

"How many visitors cards have been signed?"

"How many souls have been saved?"

"What's the capacity of this auditorium?"

"If you're not growin', you're just blowin'!"

What in the world does this type of mindset have to do with the true Kingdom of God? The short answer is: virtually nothing. Many pastors teach with alliteration using a letter of the alphabet for each of the main points of their sermons. If they taught on the theme of the letter "B," the topics of emphasis would be *bodies, buildings, and budgets*!

It is not the Lord's will to pressure believers to compel them to give tithes and offerings, regardless of the intended use. In Alabama a preacher might be prone to share the following solicitation for funds, albeit with a Southern flair of liberty and mispronunciation, *"Roll your <u>Tides</u> and your <u>Auburns</u> into the Lord's storehouse!"* [If you don't get the bad joke, you've probably never followed college football in the Southeastern Conference.]

Leaders of the Church should simply make note of the opportunity to participate and the scriptural principles of generosity. Harassing people to give money is extremely common in many Western churches and ministries, and especially so on television. Often the ministers are quick to point out that we Believers are no longer under the Law, but rather under grace in the New Covenant. They are equally quick to become legalistic over the one issue of the Old Covenant Law that is conveniently self-serving for their agenda -- i.e. tithing. It is presented as an absolute mandate. Other aspects of the Torah Law may be set aside, but tithing is a *must do* law!

Pressuring others to give contributions to a local church might mean one or more of the following is true about that particular pastor:

- He doesn't trust that God will answer his prayers;
- He is corrupt and greedy;
- He is manipulative, like Jezebel;
- He lacks discipline in his life, and wants to make a quick buck;
- He is competitive and views large numbers as an affirmation;
- He lacks Godly rest;
- He doesn't follow the principle of *"not by might, nor by power, but by My Spirit says the Lord"*;
- His personal desires exceed God's allotted portion to him at present; and/or
- He truly believes that tithing is a mandatory Torah "law" applicable for today.

That being said, are you generous to give into ministries that have high returns on investment with significant impacts strategically within the nations? Few churches or ministries ever approach a high level of influence or impact. With sufficient funding, strategic Kingdom gains could be attained through: (1) supporting affordable indigenous foreign ministers, for instance within the 10/40 Window; (2) providing micro-loans to small businesses owned by disciples in the Third World; and (3) contributing to apostolic-prophetic ministries with servant-like leadership.

I am disheartened by folks who choose to give so much money to church campaigns for building modern "cathedrals" worth tens of millions of dollars, payroll for a huge staff, recreation centers, their "own" local televised services, and marketing themselves to increase membership. Yet, at the same time, there are ministries of high impact desperate for funds that operate at very low cost and with little or no overhead costs.

Someone with any degree of success in business or investments can say with confidence, *"Show me the money!"* A wise investor does not just throw down money on any opportunity. A wise investor researches the available options and desires to have maximal bang-for-the-buck impact. Yet, many donors are deceived by their own self-serving interests or lack of knowledge. It is not a good Kingdom economic principle when a superior ministry-investment choice is available as an alternative to a poor one. That is not wise. We shall be accountable for how we invest our tithes and offerings into the Kingdom of God. And the Kingdom of God is not the same thing as the local church. [Note: There is *no Biblical mandate* for self-serving "storehouse tithes" to the local congregation, even though local congregations and leaders are deserving of "some" level of support.]

In the book of Acts believers' donations went to the feet of anointed apostolic-prophetic leadership. They were commissioned with the responsibility of using and administering it wisely. Do we place our money at the feet of anointed apostolic-prophetic leaders today? Now that is a $64,000 question! Placing funds at the feet of the prophetic Apostles in Acts is suggestive of paying honor and respect before a "ruler." It means that the donor recognizes God's anointing upon the apostolic-prophetic, foundation-building leaders. "At their feet" might also infer the funds are entrusted to those who travel on Kingdom business. Apostles are "sent ones" or messengers. They are the leaders of the "witnesses", the disciples who were willing to suffer and die as martyrs for the Cross of Jesus. So, the true apostolic-prophetic leaders are to be honored and funded. That means that the donor should have discernment as to whom the genuine apostolic-prophetic leaders are, and that the donors must trust the leaders to operate with integrity and frugality.

In the ideal world funding of genuine apostolic-prophetic leadership can be accomplished via local churches, at least in part. But recognize that there is a major conflict between a "church-centered philosophy" and a "Kingdom-centered philosophy". The local church congregation has its own self-seeking interests, regardless of how much Kingdom impact they have. They are interested in their own facilities, programs, and staff, and the maintenance of their own heritage. So, in large part, they just *assume* that 100% of what they do is just fine with the Lord. They just assume that what they do within the "church" is synonymous with accomplishing the work of the Kingdom. Well, it often isn't. They need to be accountable for frugality and maximizing impact in the global Kingdom. For instance, spending a million dollars on a crystal chandelier in a local church sanctuary is highly unlikely to have *any* Kingdom impact. There is a further complication. Existing local churches often don't want to recognize real apostolic-prophetic leaders. For one reason, the leaders of these congregations are protecting their own livelihoods. In addition the leaders might not want to become accountable and open to correction and exhortation from apostolic-prophetic leaders. And for yet another reason, most leaders like power and they are often unwilling to yield power to another. Thus, there is a great chasm between what should be done and what is actually being done today.

The major take-home lesson is: Give generously into the Kingdom of God, but learn to be discerning, through wisdom and revelation (see Ephesians 1:17), of what is the *legitimate* Kingdom of God. Otherwise, you could be unintentionally funding the enemy's plans to steal from deserving men and women in need.

PART II
Ear-Tickling Messages

For the time will come when men will not put up with sound doctrine. Instead, to suit their own desires, they will gather around them a great number of teachers to say what their itching ears want to hear. They will turn their ears away from the truth and turn aside to myths. (2 Timothy 4:3-4)

It is obvious that we now live in a season like that predicted by the Apostle Paul nearly two millennia ago. This is a season where comfort-seeking people attract to themselves teachers-of-comfort, who in turn will provide them with pleasant ear-tickling messages. The hearers don't want the truth if there is going to be any pain, correction or trial involved. They only want to hear the truth if they anticipate it will be pleasant and encouraging to hear.

People want to believe whatever suits them. People want to define theology in terms that best suit their own interests – a "god" of their own making. People want Universalism. They say, *"You go ahead and define 'god' as you will, but I'll define 'god' as I will,"* – to each his own. People want to pick and choose the attributes of their "god." People don't want supernatural transcendent truth unless it reinforces their own preconceived ideas of morality and theology. People want a man-made or woman-made morality of the moment. People just want their ears tickled!

Should we be surprised that *half-truths* are broadcast far and wide by the leaders and followers of Christianity today? Dishonesty and deception are as old as the hills. The manifestations are manifold:

- *Passing the buck* and running away from responsibility

- Exaggerating the merits and diminishing the defects…all too common in "marketing"
- Misleading information
- Suppression of information
- Fraudulent documents
- Deceptive testimony to the police and within the court room
- Lawsuits without a justifiable basis
- Slandering others with partial truths
- Ripping off the Internal Revenue Service
- Passive-aggressive *smilin' while lyin' through your teeth*
- Bribing others to avoid punishment
- Jumping the queue in front of others
- Calling sins as "mistakes"
- And, the list goes on and on and on!

As a Ph.D. scientist, one might expect that I would have observed a high standard of honest dealings within professional settings in academia and industry. However, on many occasions I've observed that scientists who pride themselves as the "champions of truth" are often overtly biased. And, these biases affect their presumptions, theories, conclusions, and world-views. There are many reasons for these less-than-honorable behaviors by scientists, for instance:

- One might fiercely defend a "pet theory" by using intentional bias in the inclusion and exclusion of facts;

- One might *"preach to the choir"* to receive a favorable opinion from one's peers whose ears are being tickled, in order to remain competitive within one's field of study and to obtain grant funding and accolades;

- One might be a sycophant seeking to curry favor from one's superiors or experts in the field, and be willing to compromise the truth for the sake of convenience;

- One might lack the courage to stand alone for the truth against a united fortified wall of resistance…it is hard to stand alone; and

- One might want to protect his or her personal income, so one will "play politics" rather than pursue the truth. I've heard it said, *"Do you know why office politics are so vicious? It is because the stakes are often so low."* That which is insignificant is elevated from mediocrity to some exaggerated level of importance.

I have personally witnessed examples of these cowardly dishonest behaviors within the science community. Dishonesty and *half-truths* aren't limited to science. The same could be said of other professions. We see similar parallels within Wall Street, Capitol Hill, corporate boardrooms, drug "doping" by professional athletes, and scandalous miscarriages of justice by the police and courts. Dishonesty, deception, and the lack of integrity are pandemic today. People have become so self-oriented. We're talking about sin and selfishness that motivates dishonesty in various forms.

These issues have grown into gigantic pervasive problems not only in the secular realm, but are at the core of many of the problems of Christianity today. These types of behaviors should not even be mentioned among ourselves as followers of Christ Jesus. These sins are simply evidences of an immature un-crucified life that is typical of our day.

Should this surprise us? A recent Barna survey in the USA indicated that only 16% of adults are considered to be "Captive Christians", which would mean devout or adhering to some Biblical Christian norms, whereas 66% were categorized as "Casual Christians" (Seven Faith Tribes: Who They Are, What They Believe, and Why They Matter; George Barna; 2009). The latter group refers to those who are nominal ("in name only"), occasional, or inconsistent with Biblical Christian norms. I would even speculate that among the 16% characterized as "Captive Christians" many are merely "religious", but have no saving knowledge and personal relationship with the Savior Jesus. Such is the season we're living in today.

And the statistics keep rolling in with evidence of growing "darkness" at least within North America and Europe. Consider the words of Isaiah, *"Arise, shine, for your light has come, and the glory of the LORD rises upon you. See, <u>darkness covers the earth and thick darkness is over the peoples</u>, but the LORD rises upon you and his glory appears over you. Nations will come to your light, and kings to the brightness of your dawn."* (Isaiah 60:1-3; emphasis added). However, if we'll rise up and speak the truth in love, then our light can pierce through this canopy of darkness! But, we must embrace the truth.

3

Locusts and Wild Honey

❧

"John's clothes were made of camel's hair, and he had a leather belt around his waist. His food was locusts and wild honey." (Matthew 3:4)

Let's contemplate the visual "message" of John-the-baptizer in order to appreciate the symbolic significance of "locusts and wild honey". It is recorded of this great prophet, *"His food was locusts and wild honey."* (Matthew 3:4b). The diet of John-the-baptizer, clad like a burden-bearing camel of the desert, provides a meaningful symbol about negative and positive words.

John was a prophet, and as such he must speak the truth at all times. That means to say it the way it is. Locusts represent destruction of life, tearing down and consuming living plants. Wild honey speaks of the fruit of flowering plants and of life in general. They are opposites. One speaks of curses, the other of blessings. What entered John's mouth would also come back out symbolically as hard words and sweet words.

Coincidentally, Torah-observant Jews were permitted to eat locusts (grasshoppers), as odd or as rare as that might seem to us today. God made provision for His people to eat certain types of insects (see Leviticus 11:20-22). We can speculate that this was because during times of locust infestations many of the crops would be destroyed. The people would need nutritious sources of protein to survive, and this is especially true for desert dwellers, for whom food is already scarce. The Scriptures do not limit John from eating things other than grasshoppers and honey. It just says that his diet included those two items. There are places in the Third World today where people eat grasshoppers.

John-the-baptizer rebuked the Pharisees and Sadducees declaring, *"You brood of vipers! Who warned you to flee from the coming wrath? Produce fruit in keeping with repentance. And do not think you can say to yourselves, 'We have Abraham as our father.' I tell you that out of these stones God can raise up children for Abraham. The ax is already at the root of the trees, and every tree that does not produce good fruit will be cut down and thrown into the fire."* (Matthew 3:7-10). There is no honey in those words. Do you recognize the similarity to Jesus' words to the proud religious folks and toward the fig tree? Both lacked fruit and deserved rebuke (see John 15 regarding bearing fruit). These words of John-the-baptizer are strikingly similar curses upon the unfruitful religious leaders.

Today we hear ministers proclaim, *"Just give me the sugar-sweet honey; just give me the blessing; just give me prosperity; just give me the pleasant things of life!"* Yet, the *Whole Counsel of the LORD* sets an entirely different standard. We need both honey and locusts, not just honey alone. *"If you find honey, eat just enough – too much of it, and you will vomit."* (Proverbs 25:16). *"It is not good to eat too much honey..."* (Proverbs 25:27a). Too much honey makes one sick. It is not good for anyone to have *only* honey. The take-home lesson is this -- both Jesus and John-the-baptizer spoke locust and honey words! We need both *locusts and honey.*

"All Scripture is God-breathed and is useful for <u>teaching</u>, <u>rebuking</u>, <u>correcting</u>, and <u>training</u> in righteousness, so that the man of God may be thoroughly equipped for every good work." (2 Timothy 3:16; emphasis added). Saying these necessary tough words is also commended to us in the following chapter – *"<u>Preach</u> the Word; be prepared in season and out of season; <u>correct</u>, <u>rebuke</u> and encourage—with great patience and careful instruction."* (2 Timothy 4:2; emphasis added). I don't know if you have ever though about it, but the Apostle Paul is talking about using the logos Word (i.e.,

the Scriptures) to share clear *negative* "locust" words with others. Rebuking and correcting are never fun! And at times, preaching, teaching, and training can be tough. These actions are not *honey* words. They are meant to bring alignment to the truth. And for that matter, in many cases so are teaching and training words. I don't know how much you are accustomed to doing it, but I've always found rebuking and correcting to be *locust* words. And this is what Paul admonished Timothy, whom he mentored.

It seems that the comforts and affluence of the West have produced a modern theology that conveniently disposes of any *negative* aspects to God's character or His prophetic purposes. Many folks just chop up the pie and discard the pieces that they don't like. Some stand firm by repeating Psalm 91 loudly, saying that *no harm* shall ever befall anyone in a "name it, claim it" manner. This selectivity can make someone resemble an ostrich burying its head in the sand of denial. The "ostrich" looks at only the pleasant passages of Scripture.

There are adverse consequences of overlooking or suppressing the "benefits" of suffering, hardship, chastisement, reproof, rebuking, etc. For the joy and glory set before Him, Jesus endured the shame and pain of being hung naked upon the Cross (see Hebrews 12:2). He looked to the future benefits.

PLEASURE VS. SORROW
[ANONYMOUS AUTHOR]

I walked a mile with Pleasure,
She chattered all the way;
But left me none the wiser,
For all she had to say.

I walked a mile with Sorrow,
And ne'er a word said she;
But, oh, the things I learned from Sorrow
When Sorrow walked with me!

—

One consequence of overlooking the benefits of hardship and training is that many of us have coincidentally de-emphasized the *Fear of the LORD* and reverence for His *Awesomeness*. We merely make the Almighty appear to be our "buddy." Sorry, but the Sovereign El Shaddai is not our pal or buddy! That is poor theology. Another consequence of overlooking the benefits of hardship and training is that some people often become bitter and disappointed when their reliance on the *name it, claim it* approach doesn't yield their anticipated result. Disappointments and delays are tough realities, and I have yet to meet a single adult who has entirely escaped from disappointments, delays, and difficulties. When they are let down, these individuals can lose hope. It can be devastating. It can cause a detour for decades in a walk of faith. Some even abandon God altogether along the journey.

While in worship I sensed the Holy Spirit prompting me to identify with Jesus' many sufferings with the phrase *"Would you stand by Me?"* As I meditated an improvisational song rose up within my spirit connecting to Jesus' pain and suffering:

WOULD YOU STAND BY ME...

...when I fasted in the desert for forty days?

...when my own mother and brothers considered me to be crazy?

...when casual followers deserted me?

...when I touched the skin of lepers?

...when the miraculously healed didn't even stop to give thanks?

...when a legion of demons spoke to me in the graveyard?

...when my hometown had no faith in me?

...when I publicly denounced the proud religious leaders?

...when the angry mob pushed in and shouted, "Stone him"?

...when John-the-baptizer was in prison and became unsure about me?

…when I had no place to rest my head at night?

…when I rode into town on a donkey?

…when Judas denied his intentions to betray me?

…when I stood before Caiaphas and the Sanhedrin?

…when they spit in my face?

…when they struck me with clenched fists?

…when they stirred up the crowd to cry "Crucify him"?

…when the prophetic rooster crowed?

…when the fury of Hell was released against me?

…when the thorns pierced my scalp?

…when many of my followers deserted me?

…when they demanded that a free man be murdered and a murderer be freed?

…when I shouted King David's words, "My God, why have you forsaken me?

…when I was slain by mere men?

…when the ground trembled beneath my pierced limbs?

…when my breathless body was carried to the tomb?

…when many doubted what they had formerly believed about me?

Would you stand by Me…

…when I come again as the Lion of Judah to rule?

…when I come seated not on a donkey, but on a white horse?

…when many realize that the 'Day of the Lord' is a terrible day?

…when all things concealed by darkness will be exposed by piercing light?

…when the kingdoms of men will be judged by the Kingdom of God?

…when I declare to many "Away from me you evil-doers, I never knew you."?

…when I separate the sheep from the goats?

...when I clear the threshing floor, gathering the grain, and burning the chaff?

...when the Redeemed all assemble before Me in radiant glory?

I ask you -- Would you stand by Me?

Looking at it from the other direction, some other individuals are imbalanced in the converse manner. They deny that the Bible says anything about prospering. They focus on the chastisement and suffering, while denying that Jesus came to give us an abundant life and the power of the Holy Spirit to work miracles. The former condition is common among Charismatic and Pentecostal denominations, whereas the latter is common among Catholic, Orthodox, Protestant, and Evangelical denominations. Let us not err by falling into either ditch, neither the one on the left side or the right side of the road. We should not view the two ends of the spectrum – suffering vs. prosperity – as mutually exclusive. This apparent paradox represents two truths at the same time. Not as an *either/or*...rather as a *both/and*. Let both sets of truths be woven into the fabric of our understanding.

It is my prayer that you heed this warning. Seek balance in this issue. We need both the *Word* and the *Spirit*. We need both the *logos* and the *rhema* word of God. And, we need both the teachings on *prosperity* as well as the teachings on *suffering*. We need balanced teachings on the multiple faces and attributes of God. Aberrant theology produces deceived believers, who in turn propagate a message of partial truths. The devil loves to present us with partial truths in order to get us to accept a larger package tainted with error. We need the *whole* counsel of God.

The American President Abraham Lincoln knew well of the "duality" of the personality traits of the Almighty. He considered that some of the ills the United States was suffering in the mid-19th century were due to the fact that American citizenry had forgotten the Creator. Lincoln recognized that God judges not only individuals, but also institutions, governments, and nations. But today, most politicians have no concept that God judges peoples and nations.

If our theology is in error, then it can become the quicksand that sinks us during times of crisis. It will not be sufficient to answer our cries for understanding and hope during times of need. Not only will it give us misleading or false answers, but it can also be the actual cause of some of the hopelessness. For instance, if my theology says to me *"God never judges or exhibits harshness or wrath,"* then I can become misled into thinking that there will be no consequences to sin. In this scenario, one sees only the Abba Daddy Father, the soft fuzzy white lamb Jesus, and the comforter Holy Spirit. Since I'm *forgiven*, this limited theology of *Abba Daddy* leads me to believe there will be no consequence or judgment upon my sin, or the sin of my family, or the sin of my city, or the sin of my nation.

Have you ever noticed that God has myriad numbers of angels, some of whom have been assigned the jobs of executing judgments? Odd as it may seem to you, some angels have the job of killing men at God's command, and in one instance a single angel of the Lord killed 185,000 men (2 Kings 20:35; Isaiah 37:36). We don't want to mess with angels.

Do you think that after Jesus rose from the grave that all angels ceased doing their assigned jobs — just because we had entered the "New Testament era?" My brothers and sisters, God <u>still</u> holds us accountable for sin. He still judges men and women. He didn't stop testing, chastising, and rebuking just because Jesus rose in glory two millennia ago. The epistle of Paul to the Romans (in the New Testament) indicates that *"the wages of sin is death."* This being true in the Church Era, then the Almighty is still a God of judgment. There are still consequences for sin. Forgiveness is possible, but consequences can linger.

Oftentimes the reason we are in a state of difficulty is because we are receiving the consequences for our own sins. We would love to just pass the buck as if we were not responsible for many of the conflicts and hardships we endure. It is my opinion, based largely upon the book of Proverbs, that some hardships in life are due to our sins (or those of family or nation in aggregate). Peter wrote, *"If you suffer, it should not be as a murderer or thief or any other kind of criminal, or even as a meddler."* (1

—

Peter 4:15). Suffering for the sake of Christ is one thing, but suffering for selfish sin is quite another.

We've grown to be effective at denying personal responsibility. We blame other people, the government, our education, our upbringing. We just want to hang it all on others and not believe our struggles may be the consequences of sin. It is easy to develop a "victim mindset" and pass the buck. Oh! When are we going to wake up to the reality that God still judges each and every one of us for our righteousness (i.e., doing what is right) or its opposite, "wrong-eousness." Let's face the facts. We're often in trouble because we deserve to be in trouble. The first step toward recovery from a difficulty is to honestly reflect on *"How did I get here?"*

Let's consider an intentionally overt example. I could choose a variety of sin habits, but this one will effectively make the point. A homosexual man is living for the moment, going to parties and exercising with regularity to produce well-defined muscles. He is sleeping around frequently with whomever he finds acceptable. One of his sins, homosexual sex, produces an environment in which he will likely suffer harm in all three dimensions of his life -- body, soul, and spirit.

First, we easily recognize the potential to suffer physical harm within his *body*. He could become infected by a sexually transmitted disease, such as HIV. It could have ravaging effects upon his immune system and, if untreated, could kill him (as is common in the Third World). This disease could be propagated to other individuals, his so-called "partners."

In his *mind*, he'll be faced with numerous mental conflicts related to his sexual and cultural identity. He'll attempt to rationalize the roles for men vs. women, for fathers vs. mothers, for masculine vs. feminine, and for marriage between a man and a woman vs. two homosexuals. He might succumb to the potential for addiction to homosexual pornography. All of which are due to short-lived inappropriate sinful habits and driven by lust. The sin choices have many ramifications. Counterfeit relationships cannot replace the *real* thing. How will he deal with guilt, acceptance, rejection, or denial…all as a result of his pattern of sin? Will he not only embrace homosexuality, but also go beyond that and reject those individuals and institutions he considers to be in opposition to his choices, such as Evangelical churches? Will they become his enemies?

In his *spirit*, he'll become an abomination to the righteous Holy Spirit as he embraces habitual sin if he doesn't repent. Without much effort he can easily become captive to the enslaving influence of a literal demon, one that is harboring and empowering homosexual sin. Oh yes, demons are real! Homosexuality is driven by a demonic force. This demonic power has a far greater enslaving power than a mere mental or physiological urge. Demons will speak to his mind and emotions to embrace homosexual sin. They will tell him to flee from the "light" of the righteous Holy Judge. The Scriptures are clear that, by his choices to live in a homosexual lifestyle, he would coincidentally be choosing to reject the saving grace of Jesus Christ, who died for him. A life that embraces the habit of this sin is incompatible with a life in the Kingdom of God…they cannot mix. The consequences of this man's sin choices are myriad -- body, mind, and spirit!

And the impact of his sin doesn't stop with him alone. The consequences of sin choices extend to those men with whom he has sexual and emotional relationships. It extends to those in his family and other relationships who are influenced by him. Perhaps if he is influenced by a literal demon of homosexuality, he will subject his "partners" to the same demonic reality that has enslaved him. The consequences to society at large are great. It will damage the God-intended meaning of the nuclear family. Perhaps he'll advocate for government policies to favor his sin choices and to restrict the freedom of expression of those who oppose his perversion. He wants the crowd to commend him, rather than to elevate his sense of guilt. If many people will side with him, he'll begin to believe the lie that he has been vindicated. Perhaps he'll request special status or special treatment from his employer due to his distinct behavior.

He believes he's a free man, when in fact he's nothing more than a slave to sin. And, his sin will become a stench in the nostrils of the Almighty. Will this go unnoticed by God? Because of his own choices to sin repeatedly, he stands under judgment now on earth. In his future the judgments of righteousness will follow him with eternal consequences. Only by the long-suffering mercy of God Almighty is he spared from the most severe punishment at present.

He needs the Savior. He needs the Deliverer. He needs the Healer. But, in order to meet the Savior, he must present himself on God's terms. He must first acknowledge his own sin. He must repent, and "must" is not optional. The on-ramp to recovery requires it! He must turn from his former ways and embrace the forgiveness and restoration only available by the power of Jesus. In all likelihood it will not be an easy journey. But, if he repents, then hope will be graciously granted to him.

Now some of you might be thinking, I don't have that particular sin in my life. But friends, we *all* are sinners. We *all* fall short of God's standard of perfection. None of us fully appreciates the thin veneer of protection provided to us by the long-suffering compassionate mercy of the Almighty. If we are not covered by the blood of Jesus, and if He were to gently lift a finger in disappointment, then angelic judgment could be rapidly dispatched. Our sin's consequences would be fully manifested instantly. We would certainly perish in less than a heartbeat. Let us not take Him or His righteousness for granted! There has been an over-emphasis on the *God-of-love* by the "churches" of the West. We must be reminded of the converse truths that speak of His impeccable character, which also include the *righteous God-of-judgment.*

If you are in a pattern of sin and merely want a feel-good pat on your back to commiserate with you during your times of depression and hopelessness, you're not going to find it here. If the cause of your demise is your own sin, then I plead with you to acknowledge your sin and repent *now.* Ask Jesus to forgive you of your sin, and *turn away* from it. I'll repeat for emphasis -- serious problems we face in life are often due to our own sins. And, if we don't abandon them, something worse will likely happen. God loves us so much that he often uses difficult circumstances to discipline us *so that* we'll turn away from our sinful habits and return to Him.

If, however, the cause of your present difficulty is not related to your own sin, then may God be merciful to you during the times of the testing of your faith. May you learn the lessons that He is imparting to you through adversity, chastisement, and suffering.

LET BALANCED REVELATION PREVAIL

The contemporary teachings of prosperity and the "nice God" concept often advocated in many Western churches must be balanced by the teachings of suffering experienced commonly in the Church of the Third World. As we hear or read the Word, we must be careful like a Berean to investigate the intended depth of meaning. Nehemiah shares a similar sentiment, *"They read from the Book of the Law of God, making it clear and giving the meaning so that the people would understand what was being read."* (Nehemiah 8:8). We must cling to one truth already known in one hand, yet while grasping an entirely new revelation in the other hand.

In the late 1970's I recorded in the cover of my Bible the following anonymous poem entitled *What God Hath Promised*. Here it is for your reflection:

> *God hath not promised skies always blue,*
> *flower-strewn pathways all our lives through.*
> *God hath not promised sun without rain,*
> *joy without sorrow, peace without pain.*
> *God hath not promised, we shall not know*
> *toil and temptation, trouble and woe.*
> *He hath not told us we shall not bear*
> *many a burden, many a care.*

But God hath promised strength for the day,
rest for the laborer, light for the way,
grace for the trials, help from above,
unfailing sympathy, undying love.

THE SUFFERING OF THE APOSTLE PAUL

During the First Century, the Apostle Paul was continuously receiving rhema revelation of the Holy Spirit about warnings and dangers on the path ahead of him. Yet, he had to walk straight into the adversities that he knew were just around the next corner (see Acts 20:22-24). Sometimes rhema words warn us to bolster our courage to face our fears.

Furthermore, we need to be quick to show patience, long-suffering mercy, and engage in intercessory prayer. Likewise, we must be slow to pronounce judgments. That is consistent with His character. But *slow-to-judgment* is not *no-to-judgment!*

There are ample instances in the Old and New Testaments where prophets or apostles released Holy Spirit-led power that resulted in tragic circumstances for the beholder. For instance, the Red Sea consuming Pharoah's army in the Old Testament and the prophetic release of death upon dishonest Ananias and Sapphira in the New Testament. Yet, God was definitely behind each of these adverse actions! Isn't the Crucifixion another fine example? *"Indeed Herod and Pontius Pilate met together with the Gentiles and the people of Israel in this city to conspire against your holy servant Jesus, whom you anointed. They did what your power and will had decided beforehand should happen."* (Acts 4:27-28; emphasis added).

How about Saul, who was redeemed as the Apostle Paul? *"But the Lord said to Ananias, 'Go! This man [Saul] is my chosen instrument to carry my name before the Gentiles and their kings and before the people of Israel. I will show him how much he must suffer for my name."* (Acts 9:15-16; emphasis added). Why must Paul suffer? One answer might be to refine him to become a different type of leader. Another answer might be to humble him and burn away his self-sufficiency. Is it possible that to some extent this amounted to a form of punishment for the murderous actions Saul had committed toward the followers of Jesus? Is it possible that Paul was reaping some of what he had sown as a zealous persecutor on behalf of the religious Pharisees? I'm not sure. Regardless, God's intention was directed at training Paul for the "greater good" of the nascent Church.

The Lord said that Paul *must* suffer, so now consider all the hardships Paul experienced:

> *"Are they servants of Christ? (I am out of my mind to talk like this.) I am more. I have worked much harder, been in prison more frequently, been flogged more severely, and been exposed to death again and again. Five times I received from the Jews the forty lashes minus one. Three times I was beaten with rods, once I was stoned, three times I was shipwrecked, I spent a night and a day in the open sea, I have been constantly on the move. I have been in danger from rivers, in danger from bandits, in danger from my own countrymen, in danger from Gentiles; in danger in the city, in danger in the country, in danger at sea; and in danger from false brothers. I have labored and toiled and have often gone without sleep; I have known hunger and thirst and have often gone without food; I have been cold and naked. Besides everything else, I face daily the pressure of my concern for all the churches. Who is weak, and I do not feel weak? Who is led into sin, and I do not inwardly burn? If I must boast, I will boast of the things that show my weakness."* (2 Corinthians 11:22-30).

God Himself decided in advance to subject Jesus and Paul to suffering. It was God's will that each undergo hardship and training for a higher purpose! *"During the days of Jesus' life on earth, he offered up prayers and petitions with loud cries and tears to the one who could save him from death, and he was heard because of his reverent submission. Although he was a son, he learned obedience from what he suffered and, once made perfect, he became the source of eternal salvation for all who obey him and was designated by God to be high priest in the order of Melchizedek.* "(Hebrews 5:7-10).

Suffering can produce a beneficial outcome. *"Therefore, since we have been justified through faith, we have peace with God through our Lord Jesus Christ, through whom we have gained access by faith into this grace in which we now stand. And we rejoice in the hope of the glory of God. Not only so, but we also rejoice in our sufferings, because we know that suffering produces perseverance; perseverance, character; and character, hope. And hope does not disappoint us, because God has poured out his love into our hearts by the Holy Spirit, whom he has given us."* (Romans 5:1-5). When we have processed our painful experiences correctly they can yield genuine hope, which is the assurance and positive attitude that God's sovereign plan is wholesome and beneficial. Paul clearly recognized the benefits of suffering, and he wrote about this topic often in his Epistle letters.

This concept is also clearly noted in the Old Testament, for instance, *"It was good for me to be afflicted so that I might learn your decrees."* (Psalm 119:71), and in the prophecy concerning the future Messiah, *"Yet it was the LORD's will to crush him and cause him to suffer, and though the LORD makes his life a guilt offering, he will see his offspring and prolong his days, and the will of the LORD will prosper in his hand."* (Isaiah 53:10). Paul was trained as a Pharisee and would likely have been familiar with these passages.

I am a firm believer that God still miraculously heals today through the power of the Holy Spirit. In fact I have participated in healing prayer with some success (see James 5:14-16). However, sickness still abounds. Even in the first century at the start of the Christian church era, there were multiple examples of disciples of Jesus having ailments. For specific examples of spiritual leaders of the early Church affected by illnesses, the New Testament is explicit in naming:

- Paul (Galatians 4:13-14)
- Epaphroditus (Phillipians 2:25-30)
- Timothy (1 Timothy 5:23-25)

- Tabitha/Dorcas (Acts 9:36-43)

- Trophimus (2 Timothy 4:20).

Yes, my friends, even the disciples and leaders of the Church suffered from illnesses. Some "faith healers" today would tend to overlook those Scriptures out of convenience. The early Church leaders were no strangers to illnesses themselves or among the people they led (see I Corinthians 11:30 and James 5:14). In addition, many of them suffered painful violent attacks while under persecution. These undoubtedly damaged and weakened their physical bodies. The same could be said for malnourished disciples of that era, due to imprisonment, dispersion, or famine.

Even Paul suffered some *"thorn in the flesh"* that God refused to remove from him (2 Corinthians 12:7-9). There is no explicit statement of what this meant to Paul, but some students of the Bible question if the "thorn" might have been poor eyesight, as hints thereof are mentioned in other passages. Nonetheless, illnesses affected the followers of Jesus in the First Century, and still do to this day. Perhaps this awareness of illnesses and hardships contributed to Paul's encouragement to believers to be *"... patient in affliction..."* (Romans 12:12).

We have another clear example in Jesus' time where a man was afflicted with blindness for decades since birth so that God's glory could be revealed at a later time in his life. Jesus said *"but this happened so that the work of God might be displayed in his life."* (John 9:3). Yes, Jesus healed him. But, the man was also afflicted for a long time before his miraculous encounter with the Messiah.

Sometimes God permits a great deal of difficulty and/or evil to last for a long time. It builds and builds until it hits the tipping point. Then God intervenes and uses the "bad" for a "good" outcome (see Romans 8:28).

Consider the difficulties of life presented to Joseph, David, or Daniel in order to position them for "greater" purposes. In particular, Joseph's brothers meant him great harm out of their jealousy, bitterness at Joseph's prophecies, and resentment of the favor of their natural father (which was directly due to the favor of the Heavenly Father).　After being sold into slavery by his brothers Joseph found himself in Egypt crying out, *"Bummer, I'm in the pit again! Would you please send down a rescue rope?"* But Yahweh meant it *all* for Joseph's good (see Genesis 50:15-21).　God's sovereign over-arching desire was bigger than the temporary pain that Joseph was forced to endure for his own training and, ultimately, for the good of the entire future Hebrew nation.

Hallelujah, there is a tipping point at which the pendulum swings the other direction!　After the accumulation or persistence of too much "evil," God releases an abundance of redemptive "good."　His repetitive patterns of forgiveness and redemption of Israel and Judah after the accumulation of great sin over decades and centuries are revealed throughout the Torah and the Prophets.　We see this pattern time and again with the exiles taken into Egypt, Assyria, and Babylon — and then returned home.

I believe that the world has entered a serious season where the difficult circumstances we are beginning to experience will stir up the *Fear of the LORD* in many folks.　That's a very good thing.　Reliable apostolic-prophetic leaders will deliver words that release *honey* and *locust* words by the power of the Holy Spirit, just as they did during the first century.　In some cases the *locust* words will warn about or even release adversities in churches, ministries, nature, governments, businesses, and other realms… at least they will be perceived as "adversities" by many people.

I have had many personal experiences that are relevant to the issue of receiving, interpreting, and delivering *locust* words, in view of a prophetic gift granted to me by the Lord.　Disciples of Jesus need to be able to receive, interpret, and implement revelation from the Holy Spirit.　The revelations can come in a diversity of patterns, such as promptings, inner convictions, dreams, visions, etc.　That's what *rhema*, the revelatory "now" word of the Holy Spirit, is all about.

Within Path Clearer ministries we strive to *"First hear from Him; then act quickly in obedience."*　Even Jesus' mother said similar things. (See John 2:5) It is our earnest desire to not operate in presumption, but to wait upon the Lord to lead. From personal experiences I concur with Leonard Ravenhill who wrote, *"A man with an experience of God is never at the mercy of a man with an argument..." (Why Revival Tarries,* Leonard Ravenhill, 1987, page 117).

Yahweh is still giving revelation to and through prophetic individuals today. Consider the words of the prophet Amos, *"Surely the Sovereign LORD does nothing without revealing his plan to his servants the prophets. The lion has roared – who will not fear? The Sovereign LORD has spoken – who can but prophesy?"* (Amos 3:7-8). And the prophet Ezekiel declared, *"...I have made you a watchman for the house of Israel; so hear the word I speak and give them warning for me."* (Ezekiel 3:17). The Old Testament prophets were followed by New Testament era prophets in the first century, the greatest of whom was the Messiah Jesus. And, God is still in the business of informing His prophetic servants today.

CONCLUSION

I realize that the theological complexity of the issues discussed above are unsettling to many. I don't pretend that I have it all worked out. It is highly unlikely that anyone does. Based on Scriptures and my personal experiences, I have some small pieces worked out, but not the entire puzzle. Regardless of the difficulties of understanding the complex truths of Scripture, we must go beyond over-simplification of theology. We must go beyond Biblical Reductionism. Maturity demands that we go beyond the easy statement, *"God is a good god, and the devil is a bad devil!"* Maturity demands that we dig deep into the written *logos* Word and learn to effectively utilize the Holy Spirit's *rhema* revelatory words.

His ways and thoughts are higher than our ways and our thoughts (see Isaiah 55:8-9). We only know in part (1 Corinthians 13:9). He knows in whole. We are mere men, albeit enabled with a measure of His power and grace to bring His Kingdom to the earth.

4

Jesus Spoke "Negative" Words

"One of the experts in the law answered him [Jesus], 'Teacher, when you say these things, you insult us also.'" (Luke 11:45)

Almost everyone is quick to acknowledge that Jesus was compassionate and filled with love. He could be merciful and tender to someone who was about to be healed of an illness. Jesus was friendly toward a crowd of despised "sinners". In addition, He was endearing to small children. However, just because Jesus was compassionate in those settings does not preclude him from being entirely different in attitude and action toward some other groups of people. Speaking as a genuine prophet Jesus comforted the afflicted and He afflicted the comforted.

Jesus was a full manifestation of the Godhead while either blessing or cursing. *"What!?"* you ask yourself *"What in the world did Jesus have to do with cursing? Whoa! That can't be right. That doesn't sound like the Jesus I recall from Sunday School."*

I'll offer a few clear examples: Jesus cursed a fig tree once, and He also cursed the Pharisees, Sadducees, and Herodians – who were esteemed for their seemingly great intelligence, influence, and honor in society. Jesus was *both* a nice guy and a tough guy at the same time! He spoke both pleasant blessings and harsh curses. At one moment Jesus praised His close friend Peter for comprehending a new revelation of the anointed

Messiah's identity. And the next moment, Jesus was rebuking the manifestation of Satan's influence in Peter's words.

Jesus was not a monolithic man of *only* sweet grace and mercy, though He had those traits to the full measure. He was both compassionate to the humble and a controversy-prone radical challenger of the proud "religious" establishment at the same time. He was not afraid to confront the demonic spirits of religion, pride, and control operating in the religious leaders of His day.

Jesus not only spoke of the reality of Heaven, but He also spoke of the reality of Hell. The Scriptures record plenty about both places in the eternal realm. I doubt whether Jesus would recognize the trendy theology taught routinely in western Christianity today as His own. In so many ways it is fundamentally aberrant! Much of today's western Christianity has little to do with the Christ!

When presenting a Holy Spirit-inspired tough word, I have personally encountered well-meaning folks who replied, *"I reject that <u>negative</u> word in Jesus name!"* This is especially true of Charismatics and Pentecostals. It stirs within me an admixture of sadness and comic humor. If God is revealing His will and it includes declaring *negative* aspects (e.g., warnings), then who are we to reject what He is saying? I've even literally heard, *"I reject the idea of the Persecuted Church!"* Just walking around declaring how victorious one is over the devil does not overrule the fact that Jesus himself spoke negative words. Mind you, not always, but in certain circumstances, when he was opposing pride or sin.

Consider some salient examples of His tough rhetoric:

Jesus of Nazareth told His disciples, *"In this world you will have trouble."* (John 16:33). He said that his disciples would be hated by the world (see John 15:18-25) and by worldly-minded members of their own biological families for obediently following Him. He said we could not elevate love for our families above our love for God. *"If anyone comes to me and does not hate his father and mother, his wife and children, his brothers and sisters*

— yes, even his own life — he cannot be my disciple. And anyone who does not carry his cross and follow me cannot be my disciple." (Luke 14:26-27). *"I have come to bring fire on the earth, and how I wish it were already kindled! But I have a baptism to undergo, and how distressed I am until it is completed! Do you think I came to bring peace on earth? No, I tell you, but division. From now on there will be five in one family divided against each other, three against two and two against three. They will be divided, father against son and son against father, mother against daughter and daughter against mother, mother-in-law against daughter-in-law and daughter-in-law against mother-in-law."* (Luke 12:49-53). We seldom hear messages preached on these uncomfortable passages.

Jesus spoke bluntly and with explicitly negative passionate terms against the religious and quasi-political leadership of the Pharisees, the Sadducees, the elders of the Sanhedrin Council, and the quasi-Jewish Herodians. The Messiah referred to those religious leaders in derogatory terms, such as "hypocrites, blind guides, sons of hell, whitewashed tombs, blind fools, snakes, and brood of vipers". And, all of those biting terms are in a single chapter, Matthew 23! In the parallel passage of "woes" in the Gospel of Luke it is recorded, *"One of the experts in the law answered him, 'Teacher, when you say these things, you insult us also.'"* (Luke 11:45; emphasis added). They got the message! Jesus insulted them bluntly and they were clearly humiliated in public (see Luke 13:17). Jesus even referred to King Herod bluntly as a "fox" and one of his own disciples as a "devil" (see Luke 13:31-32 and John 6:70, respectively).

This passionate rhetoric from the Messiah isn't remotely close to the Pollyanna, milk toast, sugar-sweet, baby food, distorted version of Jesus' words peddled these days! These passages demonstrate a tough courageous Jesus speaking in the authority of a true prophet.

There can be no question about it -- those terms exposing the nature of the leaders of His day were intentionally provocative. Yet, it is a full manifestation of the principle of speaking truth-in-love from our Savior. Those are expressions from the Jesus few have ever seriously contemplated.

Few have meditated upon the significance of these words of Jesus, even though they're in the "red letters" of the Bible. Many who quote the familiar saying today *"What Would Jesus Do?"* cannot fathom the truth and consequences of a Jesus who spoke like that! He said He didn't come to bring peace, but rather a divisive sword and a consuming fire. For those who chose to follow His teachings and commandments, they would experience troubles including the breakup of families; turning one relative against the other.

Confrontation is necessary at times. One must tear down what is wrong in order to build up what is right. Sometimes the prophet must speak *locust* words, rather than *honey* words. Our Path Clearer ministry was established to resemble a metaphoric bulldozer uprooting, exposing, and leveling the path (See Isaiah 40:3-6). Bulldozing is disruptive, yet necessary. Once the path has been cleared of weeds, rocks, and obstacles, others who follow are then free to build upon the leveled *terra firma*. Bulldozers dig deep down to bedrock, which is capable of supporting a heavy structure. One should only build upon the truth, as anything built upon lies will have a faulty foundation.

Jesus, referring to Himself as the Chief Cornerstone said, *"The stone the builders rejected has become the capstone; the Lord has done this and it is marvelous in our eyes. Therefore I tell you that the kingdom of God will be taken away from you* [i.e., those who reject the Messiah] *and given to a people who will produce its fruit. He who falls on this stone will be broken to pieces, but he on whom it falls will be crushed."* (Matthew 21:42-44). Yet we seldom hear pastors or evangelists today mention the negative words declared by the Messiah, who came to fulfill the Law and establish the New Covenant!

Modern ministers present an image of Jesus as a sugar-sweet, nurturing, feminized, mother figure, grace-giver, in the genre of a female Middle Eastern genie-in-a-bottle (like "I Dream of Jeannie" on TV) or a Santa Claus. But, that is not the *real* Jesus. We are so misled today that we can't recognize the obvious. Yes Virginia, there is a Jesus. And, he is not the same thing as the mythical gift-giver. Yes, Jesus was a nice guy, but He was also known to fashion a whip with His own hands before violently charging into the Temple to overthrow the vendor tables of the moneychangers.

Jesus cursed a barren fig tree saying, *"May you never bear fruit again!"* (Matthew 21:19). The tree rapidly withered and shocked his disbelieving followers. So He instructed them, *"I tell you the truth, if you have faith and do not doubt, not only can you do what was done to the fig tree, but also you can say to this mountain, 'Go, throw yourself into the sea', and it will be done. If you believe, you will receive whatever you ask for in prayer."* (Matthew 21:18-22). This passage is frequently cited by those folks who are familiar with "Word of Faith" denominational teachings, and always in terms that are meant to be entirely "positive". Yet, ironically the context indicates it refers to Jesus' followers speaking *curses* of destruction. The two examples noted therein include the death of the fig tree and the displacement of the mountain. They were both *locust* words, not *honey* words. Jesus said that there is power in our faith-laden words, and in this particular passage He meant negative words spoken in authority. He was explicitly talking about curses in this particular case.

Jesus also declared to his disciples in advance that He must go to Jerusalem and suffer horribly at the hands of the Jewish and Roman officials, and then be murdered though He was innocent (see Matthew 17:21-28). Upon hearing this apparently negative prophetic word His very close friend, Peter, replied in defiant ignorance with a rebuke to Jesus. I speculate Peter's words resembled, *"No way! I reject that negative word! There won't be anyone dying on my watch! That ain't happening!"* Good intentions, but not God's plan. Jesus had the last word on this matter, as He replied in rebuke to Peter, *"Get behind me, Satan! ... You do not have in mind the things of God, but the things of men."* (Mark 8:33).

Some folks fail to recognize truths that are inconsistent with their beliefs or theological worldview. Life on earth is difficult and not fully heavenly...yet. The Persecuted Church is a reality. It is overtly present in many countries outside of the Western World. At least during this juncture in time the West is largely spared of dangerous threats. The Persecuted Church is thriving and producing real disciples of Christ elsewhere who understand the difficult "way of the Cross." They know well the truth of Joseph's declaration about his devious brothers, *"You intended to harm me, but God intended it for good to accomplish what is now being done, the saving of many lives."* (Genesis 50:20).

Denial of the truth by using the simple phrase, *"I reject that negative word,"* just because one's personal beliefs have no room for it, is not embracing the *Whole Counsel of the LORD*. *"But as for me and my household, we choose to serve the LORD."* (Joshua 24:15b). We would rather have the *whole* counsel than the *half* counsel. We don't want partial truths. We want the Old Testament and the New Testament. We want the old wine and the new wine. We want the logos Word of God and the rhema word of God, too. We want the Word and the Spirit. We want the truth and the love. We want Jesus' positive words and His negative words. We won't settle for a *half* counsel; we want the *Whole Counsel of the LORD*!

PART III
The God of Adversity

...the Lord gives you the bread of adversity and the water of affliction...
(Isaiah 30:20)

Due to the serious need to correct the all-too-common practice of Biblical Reductionism, I have decided to devote three chapters to the theme of *the God of Adversity*. Reductionism is the act of building a belief system or theology by picking and choosing only the Scriptures that one finds appealing, and thereby overlooking or suppressing other Scriptures. In the process of "distilling down" the Scriptures, vital information, revelation, and insight (often to the contrary) is left to the side of the table as scrap material.

The first of these three chapters will provide an overview, followed by two chapters of concise compilations of Scriptures from the Old Testament and the New Testament to bolster the conclusions. There is a serious need for correction and clarification among the Body of Christ pertaining to this critical topic.

5

The God of Adversity – Overview

The LORD brings death and makes alive; he brings down to the grave and raises up. The LORD sends poverty and wealth; he humbles and he exalts.
(1 Samuel 2:6-7)

Many, if not most, pastors and teachers in the West have reached an *opinion* that the God of the Bible has somehow lost many of His attributes and virtues. There has been an intentional shifting away from the attributes of God that are consistent with the "God of the Old Testament." These modern Western pastors and teachers have de-emphasized those tough characteristics, while at the same time over-emphasizing *selected* attributes of Jesus from the New Testament scriptures that seem to be more pleasant. Why has this happened?

It is highly probable that the message has been changed progressively over the decades to make the listeners more comfortable. One wouldn't want to scare away any potential members or tithers of local congregations. It just wouldn't be considered as "winsome." A more gentle and appealing Gospel-derivative has replaced some or all of the harsher, judgmental, strict, and holy attributes of God with modern sugarcoated non-offensive language. It is giving some listeners precisely what they *want to hear*, rather than what some of them *need to hear*. They don't want to see *all* of God's attributes, just the pleasant ones. Our Western society is focused on making us happy at all cost, making us content at all cost, while suppressing any contrary Biblical insights. These pastors and teachers are pleased to provide their congregations with a compromised Gospel. This new "gospel" must not erode the American self-declared entitlements to *"life, liberty, and the pursuit of happiness."*

Where did this notion come from that happiness is a *right*? When did happiness become a divine entitlement? How did we arrive at this "nice god" theology? Is the god of this new theology really an accurate representation of the God of the Bible, who is referred to as The LORD - Yahweh? Ask yourself these questions.

The selective emphasis on only His *pleasant* attributes (i.e., a friendly "buddy" god without any severity) has damaged modern theology. This new *God of unconditional love* message is destroying the truth. It is destroying the meaning of the Crucifixion on the Cross. It is replacing genuine repentance with a warm feeling of gratitude and apology. Is it really calling us to repentance…think about it? We now have a watered-down gospel-derivative message that lacks the depth of sin-removing repentance power. There is real *power* in the blood of Jesus. But in this new *nice god/buddy god* theology, why do we even need the spilled blood of Jesus for anything?

This new theology minimizes the consequences of sin and the need for genuine repentance. It just tickles the ears of an increasingly affluent pleasure-seeking society. They say, *"We don't want to hear the whole Bible preached. Just give us only the nice red letters of Jesus."* Little do they realize that a sizeable portion of the red letters of Jesus in the Gospels are in fact harsh, critical, and judgmental words demanding repentance, obedience, and holiness. Some in fact are overt curses and criticisms (see Chapter 4).

Consumerism has also become highly instrumental in avoiding the truth. Many folks just shop around for religious teachings that make them feel good but demand nothing from them. They don't care for the *whole* truth that includes both pleasant and unpleasant principles. They only want *partial* truths, and in many cases, they don't even want *any* of the truth. Our *pick-and-choose* society cannot afford to continue to treat the truth with contempt in the same way that they shop at a well-stocked supermarket for luxury items to comfort themselves. This is a serious issue.

Returning to the main point, I hear some pastors exclaim:

- *God never does anything harmful, harsh, wrathful, or judgmental.*
- *God did that in the past, but not anymore. That is an outdated view of God's character. He's not like that. We know better today.*
- *We're not under the Old Covenant; we're under the New Covenant.*
- *We're not bound by the Old Testament; we're freed by the New Testament.*
- *That sounds like the Hell, Fire, and Brimstone preaching of the past.*

These are sad misrepresentations of the intended meanings of the Old vs. New Covenants. None of the attributes of the God of Abraham, Isaac, and Jacob have changed. Yahweh is still the same God and his attributes have not altered! Although He is perceived by many to have revealed more about His "nice" nature in the New Testament and New Covenant, He has not changed! There are plenty of Hebrew (i.e., "Old" Testament) Scriptures that demonstrate the "nice" side of His attributes. This dichotomous view held by many is not correct. He is not simply a "fierce" God in the Old Testament and a "nice" God in the New Testament with mutual exclusivity. Yet, many pastor-teachers today declare this misleading dogma all the time. He has both types of attributes in the Old and New Testaments. We recognize the same ironic pairing in the familiar sentence, *"It was the best of times, it was the worst of times"* (A Tale of Two Cities, Charles Dickens).

As an exercise to bolster my own understanding of God's character, I have cataloged a lengthy list of Scripture passages that directly attributes to God an active role (if not complete responsibility) for various adversities, judgments, chastisements, plagues, famines, and severe weather. These scriptures are found throughout <u>both</u> the Old and New Testaments.

Thus, God's fierce attributes can't be merely written off as being exclusive to the "old" Hebrew Bible. Many examples of these types of explicit passages are included in the following Chapters 6 and 7. In these passages the Sovereign God of Israel says that He takes responsibility for these actions that we today would likely consider as harsh, wrathful, negative, or unloving. An exhaustive search on this topic would result in a giant list of Scriptures that would warrant an entire book devoted to just this topic (i.e., *The God of Adversity*). So a few chapters of this current book don't do this subject justice…it just opens the can of worms. Hopefully, this is a sufficient summary of numerous examples to convincingly refute the common theological error.

Suffice it to say, anyone who reads the Bible encounters innumerable examples of God's judgment, wrath, and holy righteous standards from cover to cover. It is not at all difficult to find over one hundred separate explicit examples in the Bible. Yet, many today say simplistically, *"God is a good god, and the devil is a bad devil."* Both phrases are true. But, this oversimplification of the *Whole Counsel of the LORD* does a disservice to us. If our theology is aberrant on this topic, we will likely have a poor understanding of the *Fear of the LORD*, which is the beginning of wisdom (see Proverbs 1:7). Without the *Fear of the LORD*, we can be easily deceived and lose our focus on His omnipotence, omnipresence, glory, and other attributes of His character.

There are many faces of God. Yet, we are permitting some pastors and teachers to define for us only the faces that they would like for us to see. Our Creator God manifested as *Father* is both a tender Abba "Daddy" to His children sitting on His knee, as well as a wrath-yielding righteous Judge upon the Throne. Our Creator God manifested as *Son* is both the soft sacrificial white silent lamb, as well as the roaring Lion of Judah waging war. Our Creator God manifested as *Spirit* is both the gentle Comforter-Counselor providing nourishing water, as well as an all-consuming pillar of fire to burn up the dross! Yahweh's multi-faceted attributes are revealed to those who intentionally purpose to know Him in His *fullness* of characteristics.

Unfortunately the term "Full Gospel" has been largely co-opted and roped off for a narrow purpose -- to encourage people toward a single spiritual gift, that of speaking in tongues (albeit this supernatural gift is a good thing). Thus, in this context the term "Full Gospel" is a bit misleading. Alternatively, this term could be re-used to great effect to encourage people to embrace the *Whole Counsel of the LORD*. So the terms *Full Gospel* and *Whole Counsel of the LORD* have little in common in current use.

Let us consider another damaging theological error that is common today. Some people who hold to aberrant *Replacement Theology* argue that the Old Testament (Hebrew Bible) has minimal value to us "Christians" today. In essence, to the proponents of *Replacement Theology* the New Testament has all but eradicated any value for the Jewish people and the literal land of Israel. They consider the term "Israel" to figuratively represent the "Church" today. They incorrectly presume that Christianity is a new religion that God sanctioned to replace the former old Hebraic faith of the Jews*. But, the "harsh" attributes and characteristics of God are clearly reinforced in <u>both</u> the New Testament and the New Covenant. If there was no evidence of the "harsh" attributes in the New Testament or The Church era, then the argument could be more effective. But, the Scriptural evidence is plentiful and runs to the contrary.

The LORD – Yahweh is still the God of Abraham, Isaac, and Jacob. Yahweh is still the God of the Jewish people, as well as the God of all nations. His eyes are still keenly set with affection upon Mount Zion in the physical land of Israel. Jesus lived as the Jewish Messiah, died as the Jewish Messiah, and will return again as the resurrected Jewish Messiah and Lord over all mankind (see Isaiah 53 and Psalm 22). Replacement Theology is a doctrine of demons that has infected large portions of Christianity. It seeks to undermine the Hebraic roots of the faith. If you chop off the roots, there will be no nourishment for the tree. This root-less tree will not yield fruit for the Kingdom of Heaven.

[*Although a digression from the theme of this chapter, our Father in Heaven is very concerned about the "One New Man," the union of Jewish and Gentile believers in Jesus the Messiah that will increase with the fullness of time. This concept is developed in the Epistles to the Ephesians and the Romans. The central role of the Jewish people within His Kingdom has not been abrogated, abandoned, or negated by Christianity.]*

THE GOD OF ADVERSE WEATHER

I want to share some thoughts and insights on the theology of natural disasters and adversity for us to consider. A tidy over-arching systematic theology for this topic is difficult to compile. One can easily fall in error on either side of the road. There is a ditch on the one side that says that God is *never* behind anything "adverse," such as severe weather. There is an opposite ditch that says that God is *always* behind "adverse" things, including severe weather.

Does not Scripture indicate that Yahweh causes the rain to fall on the just and the unjust? Does He not sovereignly cause and direct weather patterns, such as the cold winds of the polar caps and the warm winds of the equatorial tropics? Does He not govern rain clouds, thunderstorms, hail, and snow?

Is it possible that on the one hand the "beneficial" aspects of a thunderstorm results in praise expressed to God by one family, who earnestly desires rains for their farm, yet on the other hand is cursed by another family, who unfortunately experienced the floodwaters downstream that resulted from the same thunderstorm? Just stop one moment and think about this – doesn't the complexity of the question give you an unsettled feeling? So, let the Scriptures speak for themselves, and let us observe without bias as we consider some examples:

- *"His way is in the whirlwind and the storm, and clouds are the dust of his feet. He rebukes the sea and dries it up; he makes all the rivers run dry... The mountains quake before him and the hills melt away. The earth trembles at his presence, the world and all who live in it."* (Nahum 1:3b-5);

- *"When I shut up the heavens so that there is no rain, or command locusts to devour the land..."* (2 Chronicles 7:13a);

- *"The earth trembled and quaked, and the foundations of the mountains shook; they trembled because he was angry. Smoke rose from his nostrils; consuming fire came from his mouth, burning coals blazed out of it. He parted the heavens and came down; dark clouds were under his feet. He mounted the cherubim and flew; he soared on the wings of the wind. He made darkness his covering, his canopy around him—the dark rain clouds of the sky. Out of the brightness of his presence clouds advanced, with hailstones and bolts of lightning. The LORD thundered from heaven; the voice of the Most High resounded. He shot his arrows and scattered the enemies, great bolts of lightning and routed them."* (Psalm 18:7-14);

- *Ask the LORD for rain in the springtime; it is the LORD who makes the storm clouds...* (Zechariah 10:1a);

- *"He destroyed their vines with hail and their sycamore-figs with sleet. He gave over their cattle to the hail, their livestock to bolts of lightning. He unleashed against them his hot anger, his wrath, indignation and hostility—a band of destroying angels."* (Psalm 78:47-49);

- *"...he who made the Pleiades and Orion, who turns blackness into dawn and darkens day into night, who calls the waters of the sea and pours them out over the face of the land—the LORD is his name..."* (Amos 5:8);

- *"I form the light and create darkness, I bring prosperity and create disaster; I, the LORD, do all these things."* (Isaiah 45:7);

- *"If any of the peoples of the earth do not go up to Jerusalem to worship the King, The Lord Almighty, they will have no rain."* (Zechariah 14:17; and possibly referring to the future Millennial reign of the Messiah).

God frequently takes attribution to Himself in the Scriptures for caus-ing adverse events and judgments, and including adverse weather. This is at the core of His sovereignty. All authority in Heaven and earth has been granted to Jesus. He has vastly greater authority over the earth than does the prince of the power of the air, the devil. That bears repetition -- Jesus has greater authority on earth than the devil!

One can easily pull together a collection of more than a hundred *overt* and *explicit* Biblical passages that record that God himself does in fact *cause* certain adversities, calamities, or harsh weather. If in fact you doubt the veracity of this claim, please read carefully the examples of the Scriptures listed in the following two chapters. This is not an exhaustive list, rather just a concise compilation to underscore the truth of this conclusion.

Based on these abundant scriptures from Genesis to Malachi in the Old Testament and from Matthew to Revelation in the New Testament, this is not a *one-side-takes-all* issue (i.e., God-of-judgment in the Old Testament vs. God-of-love in the New Testament). From cover-to-cover there are explicit examples of God's active participation in adversity, as well as with compassion and mercy. From the start of mankind in Genesis to the end of man's dominion in Revelation, it is not an "either/or" situa-tion. It is a "both" situation. God's attributes include compassion, mercy, and gentleness on one side. And on the other side, His attributes include justice, judgment, and vengeance.

If you study the Scriptures you'll find more evidence for adversity (e.g., adverse weather) being attributed to God than being attributed di-rectly to the devil. Some Bible-believing Christians might have a hard time believing this fact. Their personal bias will interfere with the recog-nition of the obvious. There is a strong tendency for many people today to deny the judgment and wrath side of Biblical theology by blaming *all* adversity on the devil.

There is an opposite tendency for those of the other persuasion to not acknowledge the blessing and prospering aspects of God's characteristic attributes. The latter can err on the side of *Retribution Theology*. We seldom hear someone speaking from the position of the *Whole Counsel of the LORD*, which reflects both of these seemingly contradictory positions. We don't like that uncomfortable realm where we don't have tidy answers to life's difficult questions.

God has given specific prophetic revelation to *reliable* prophets and prophetic individuals about His intentions in certain matters (see Amos 3:6-7), such as soon-to-be-released adverse weather. I personally have experienced prophetic words from the Lord about adverse weather in the form of tornados and hurricanes.

This might just surprise you, but not every hurricane is caused by the devil! Yet, we often make attribution to the devil for adverse events that were directly from the Hand of the Lord. Just because a hurricane can threaten human lives and destroy coastal property, it can also deliver copious rainfall to replenish millions of acres of land so as to help sustain crops that can subsequently feed millions of people. A single hurricane can deliver billions of tons of water to the ground in a few days. That water nourishes humans, animals, plants, trees, fungi, bacteria…all sorts of life forms that cannot survive without moisture. In many geographic regions hurricanes are one of the major contributors, if not the predominant source, of water.

You want no hurricanes? Fine! Follow the Burger King marketing slogan and just *"Have it your way."* No hurricanes, no thunderstorms, no monsoons. That would just leave us with no plants, no animals – just barren deserts. Welcome to the Sahara!

Simply stated, based upon numerous Biblical examples, adverse weather can be caused by God, and it can also be caused by the devil. An example of the latter occurred during the testings of Job, when a tornado destroyed his home and the lives of his children. However, the preponderance of examples in the Scriptures explicitly state that God is in control as a causal agent even in the cases where the circumstances don't seem to mesh with our modern ideas of a "God of love."

Some of us are prone to quickly declare in a rough situation, *"That must be God's judgment!"* However, given that one can make a Biblical case *for* or *against* adversity in a given situation, we need to be careful to know His rhema revelation on that particular situation. In one case, His desire could be that we plead for mercy via intercession. In another similar situation, His desire could be that we accept this prophetic inevitability and adapt to the impending "adversity." His *desire* is the issue. It isn't about what you or I think. Our opinions do not matter. It is all about His sovereign will coupled to us acting in obedience upon His revelation.

As followers of Yahweh, we need to be quick to show patience, mercy, long-suffering, and humility. Likewise, we must be cautious and slow to pronounce judgments. This behavior is consistent with His own character. *"Rend your heart and not your garments. Return to the LORD your God, for he is gracious and compassionate, <u>slow to anger</u> and abounding in love, and he relents from sending calamity."* (Joel 2:13; emphasis added). But, *slow-to-anger* is not the same as *no-to-anger*! *Slow-to-judgment* is not the same as *no-to-judgment*!

As another similar example, the prophet Nahum declared, *"The LORD is a jealous and avenging God; the LORD takes vengeance and is filled with wrath. The LORD takes vengeance on his foes and maintains his wrath against his enemies. The LORD is <u>slow to anger</u> and great in power; the LORD will not leave the guilty unpunished. His way is in the whirlwind and the storm, and clouds are the dust of his feet."* (Nahum 1:2-3; emphasis added). Note in this passage that <u>both</u> aspects of God's character are explicitly recorded side-by-side. Yes, He is slow to anger. He is extremely patient and long-suffering. But He also displays vengeance and wrath against His enemies. Not one or the other, as many people choose to believe these days. He does not drop the one attribute in order to embrace the other. He is the purveyor of both compassion and wrath. These are inner core virtues of the Almighty, and He does not change.

There are instances in the Old and New Testaments where prophets or apostles released Holy Spirit-led power that resulted in death. Two examples of tragic outcomes include the Red Sea (or Sea of Reeds) drowning of Pharoah's army in the Old Testament (see Exodus 14) and the prophetic judgments by the Apostles resulting in the death of Ananias and Sapphira in the New Testament (see Acts 5). God was definitely behind each of these adverse actions! That is the obvious conclusion in each case.

God uses adversity and/or judgments to accomplish many purposes. But, with regard to how He treats mankind in general, we recognize two quite different categories of circumstances based upon whom He is dealing with. In the most obvious case, God waits patiently for a long season while a person, a group, or a nation progressively and overtly sins against His standards. You might refer to this as God's judgments upon His enemies.

GOD'S JUDGMENTS TOWARD HIS ENEMIES

Sin is Biblically defined as *missing the mark*. So, as individuals or groups of people continuously miss the mark and tally up lengthy lists of sins (i.e., idolatry, lawlessness, selfishness, pride, sexual perversion, etc.), the accumulative effect eventually warrants that God take action. He is a judge, and He is a patient judge. He is also a defender of the oppressed, the poor, the widow, the alien, and the orphan (see Isaiah 58). He desires to set the captives free. He will accomplish both purposes...judgment against sinners and mercy toward those He chooses.

The Almighty will not strive with stubborn men forever. Let us get one fact clearly established up front. If it were not for His mercy none of us would be alive today, for Paul wrote that, *"...all men have sinned and fall short of His glory...For the wages of sin is death..."* (Romans 3:23 and 6:23). The Bible is clear; none of us are righteous in and of ourselves. All of us have *missed the mark* and are deserving of His judgment. If it weren't for the Cross, then none of us would stand a chance.

I've got some good news and I've got some bad news. First, the bad news. *"God is just: He will pay back trouble to those who trouble you and give relief to you who are troubled, and to us as well. This will happen when the Lord Jesus is revealed from heaven in blazing fire with his powerful angels. He will punish those who do not know God and do not obey the gospel of our Lord Jesus. They will be punished with everlasting destruction and shut out from the presence of the Lord and from the majesty of his power..."* (2 Thessalonians 1:6-9).

Now, for the good news. There is a remedy offered to sinners by the Almighty. Simply stated it is one thing -- repentance. The Creator offers to the rebellious, *"Come and do it My way. Come to Me in humility. Repent. Change your heart and actions. Abandon your way and embrace My way."* Repentance is the fulcrum of the tipping see-saw, it is the hinge upon which our fate is determined. If we in pride say, *"I'll do it my way,"* then our eternal fate is assured to be hellish by our obstinance. If however we humbly say, *"I'll do it His way,"* then our eternal fate is assured to be blissful by our surrender.

Returning to the issue at hand, He gives men a long leash, but He eventually pulls back and jolts their necks! Depending on the sin and circumstances, His leash can last for weeks, months, years, decades, centuries, and even millennia. There are many citations in the Bible where God says that after a long time of waiting He will eventually reach a point where the scales have tipped "against" someone or a group of people. When that happens, He even says to some of his followers, *"It is too late. Don't even pray for them anymore!"* (paraphrased from Jeremiah chapters 7, 14, and 15). So, here we clearly see the "Judge" coming through, as He eventually holds people accountable for having missed His standard. Thus there will be consequences, and they will be adverse. People will reap what they have sown. If they have sown plenty of sin without repentance, then the consequences are assured. We see this pattern repeated throughout the Bible.

During the early 18th Century, the Great Awakening of the United States was fueled by passionate preaching concerning the reality of judgment and hell. Most noted for leading this call toward repentance was the pastor-preacher-author Jonathan Edwards. He delivered the infamous sermon *"Sinners in the Hands of an Angry God"* in 1741. In a biography of Edwards' life, Ralph Turnbull wrote that Edwards was, *"a man who proclaimed the whole counsel of God, not shunning the difficult and unpopular themes of revelation."* (*Jonathan Edwards: The Great Awakener*, Helen K. Hosier, 1999; page 173; emphasis added).

This great spiritual statesman spoke and wrote frequently on the Biblical themes of judgment and hell. Edwards stated, *"The unseen, unthought of ways and means of persons' going suddenly out of the world are innumerable and inconceivable. Unconverted men walk over the pit of hell on a rotten covering, and there are innumerable places in this covering so weak that they will not bear their weight, and these places are not seen. The arrows of death fly unseen at noonday; the sharpest sight cannot discern them."* (*ibid*, page 92). Jonathan Edwards' appreciation for the *Whole Counsel of the LORD* and his unashamed preaching on "negative" topics such as hell and God's justice and judgment upon sinners contributed greatly to the "success" of his ministry of calling men and women to embrace genuine repentance in the 18th Century.

Repentance is the on-ramp to salvation and the entrance into the Kingdom of God. According to the author of the book of Hebrews, one of the fundamental truths of the faith is the *"...foundation of repentance from acts that lead to death..."* (Hebrews 6:1; emphasis added). Everything else rests upon this foundation. This is the starting point of a relationship with the Almighty.

Have we not noticed that the message of repentance was preached by John-the-baptizer, then by Jesus, and then by His newly commissioned apostles, and all in rapid sequence? John-the-baptizer declared, *"Repent, for the kingdom of heaven is near...Prepare the way for the Lord, make straight paths for him."* (Matthew 3:2-3; emphasis added). Then, Jesus arrived and confirmed this truth at the onset of His public ministry and declared, *"Repent, for the kingdom of heaven is near."* (Matthew 4:17; emphasis added). And, then the apostles were sent out two-by-two into the villages at Jesus' command. *"They went out and preached that people should repent."* (Mark 6:12; emphasis added). Furthermore, at the "start" of the Church at Pentecost, Peter preached to a large audience and declared, *"Repent and be baptized, everyone of you, in the name of Jesus Christ for the forgiveness of sins. And you will receive the gift of the Holy Spirit."* (Acts 2:38; emphasis added).

Do we not see this clear pattern? Listen, if the ministries of John-the-baptizer, Jesus, and the original twelve apostles all *started* with an explicit message of repentance (and the message of the Kingdom of God), don't you think we should continue this same pattern today in our evangelism? But "no," we make it so easy for people today. Just because someone raises his or her hand when all eyes are closed during prayer or privately marks a commitment card in a church gathering, and perhaps due to an emotional prompting, does not mean that the individual had genuinely repented.

It is my firm belief based upon the pattern established by John-the-baptizer, Jesus, and the Apostles that repentance is a requirement for salvation and entrance into the Kingdom. It is not optional just because it seems old fashioned. Paul and Barnabas preached that, *"We must go through many hardships to enter the kingdom of God."* (Acts 14:22). Entrance into the Kingdom is not easy, even though we're taught otherwise these days. The British writer C.S. Lewis wrote, *"...a man who admits no guilt can accept no forgiveness."* (The Problem of Pain; 1940). From Lewis' perspective, one who claims to accept Jesus yet without acknowledging one's need for forgiveness shall receive neither!

Repentance is the willful acknowledgment of the grievousness of sin that condemns one to an eternity of separation from Yahweh's presence. Repentance goes beyond remorse or shame. Remorse without repentance is common today outside of the realm of obedient disciples. Repentance is the turning point, the fulcrum upon which an individual's spiritual and eternal life hinges.

Once we turn away from sin and walk toward the Lord's holy narrow path, we must further demonstrate evidence of repentance. John-the-baptizer warned, *"Produce fruit in keeping with repentance."* (Matthew 3:8). Once we have "turned" we must continue to walk in the new direction. Prior to repentance life is all about "us". But, after repentance life is all about Him!

Without repentance, God's "hand of favor and restraint" may be lifted from an individual, group, or nation. We are absolutely dependent upon God's grace. But, if we are foolish enough to go our own way, then He may withdraw His protection, power, and presence from our lives or communities. He may give us over to our own sinful desires, as Paul described in Romans chapter one, in order that we can experience the rotten "fruit" of our sin.

This "passive" withdrawal by God's hand of restraint is symbolized in another way by God's warning through the Apostle John to the "church" of Ephesus in Revelation. *"Remember the height from which you have fallen! Repent and do the things you did at first. If you do not repent, I will come to you and remove your lampstand from its place."* (Revelation 2:5; emphasis added). A lampstand provides illumination and drives away darkness. Without repentance, one will be overcome with spiritual darkness.

Another picture is given by the prophet Zechariah, *"Then I took my staff called Favor and broke it, revoking the covenant I had made with all the nations."* (Zechariah 11:10: emphasis added). In the context of this passage the prophet made a public demonstration using a shepherd's staff that normally symbolizes authority and protection. Once it is broken, favor was lifted from the obstinate "flock."

Repentance is the key to remaining on the side of God's favor, rather than on the side of God's judgment. Someone who is unwilling to yield to God's wisdom and to repent is like voluntarily walking out from under an umbrella during a violent hailstorm. The protection and favor is lifted so that the figurative hailstorm will be a literal "hell-storm". The adverse consequences are assured. The devil's demonic army will gain more access to one's life. They'll steal, kill, and destroy without being impeded.

Lest you discount the pleading of my heart, thinking to yourself that this author is a single voice with these strange and antiquated insights on the character of the Almighty, consider three recently deceased noteworthy spiritual leaders:

First, consider the words of John White, *"He* [God] *has no joy in the death of the wicked, only an infinite pain. Yet he will do what he must. His attitude to sin is inflexible. He will not stay his hand however long he may delay it. He will warn, threaten, plead. But finally he will act, and when he does his judgments will be as thorough as they are unswerving. It has been so throughout the Scripture, throughout church history, and it will remain so till the end of time…When foreign armies overran Israel or Judah, the heads of little ones would be dashed against the rocks, the women raped, and the aged tossed over a precipice. We are sickened by the horror of it all and avoid those pages of Scripture, which implicate God's judgments in such atrocities. We prefer to worship a different god, made up of our favorite selections from Scripture."* (*The Golden Cow*, John White, Intervarsity Press, 1979, pages 158-159).

Second, consider the quickened words of Leonard Ravenhill, the fiery preacher of repentance and holiness, *"Sodom, which had no Bible, no preachers, no tracts, no prayer meetings, no churches, perished. How then will America and England be spared from the wrath of the Almighty, think you? We have millions of Bibles, scores of thousands of churches, endless preachers— and yet what sin! Men build our churches but do not enter them, print our Bibles but do not read them, talk about God but do not believe Him, speak of Christ but do not trust Him for salvation, sing our hymns and then forget them. How are we going to come out of all this?"* (*Why Revival Tarries*, Leonard Ravenhill, 1987, page 58).

Leonard Ravenhill's plea was for a passionate uncompromising level of obedience to the Lord that would result in men repenting and having their hearts of stone being replaced with hearts of flesh. He pleaded for mature spiritual leaders of holiness to rise up and to speak the *Whole Counsel of the LORD* to provoke repentance. He wanted men of faith to burn under the Holy Spirit's anointing to stimulate repentance. He wrote, *"The more fire in the pulpit, the less burning in hell-fire."* (*ibid*, page 112). These words might seem out-of-date, harsh, and not at all "seeker-sensitive" within our comfort-seeking tolerant lifestyles today. But, they are nonetheless the truth!

And finally, consider one of my acquaintances, Peter Dugulescu, one of the 20th Century courageous spiritual leaders in Eastern Europe under Communism. He lived under the brutal oppression of the Romanian dictator, Nicolae Ceausescu. As a bold preacher of the truth, Peter's murder was scheduled on several occasions by this evil regime. And several attempts were made upon his life. Following Ceausescu's demise, Peter eventually served in the Romanian Parliament. Thus, he had earned through his many travails an excellent perspective to speak into the Western world today.

In the final decade of his life, Peter preached passionate warnings among various churches in America. He wrote: *"Two thousand years ago Jesus Christ said to his disciples: 'You are the salt of the earth, you are the light of the world' (Matthew 5:13-14). I believe that the state of darkness and breakdown of a nation is inversely proportional to the church's spiritual power, to salt and illuminate the nation with the Gospel."* (*Repenters*, Peter Dugulescu, 2004, page 286). He was deeply concerned with the "darkness" that he saw rapidly developing within Amcrica.

On August 26, 2001 Peter Dugulescu declared to a group of journalists, *"America has become the most powerful and blessed nation in the world because it has honored God and chosen to be 'one nation under God'! The greatness of America comes in the first instance from the Lord, but America has departed a long way from God. If the nation does not repent and turn back God will judge it...I am not a prophet, but I tell you in the Name of the*

Lord, <u>in less than ten years</u> other pagan nations will attack and humiliate this country and America will no longer be America." (ibid, page 286; emphasis added).

Then, several nights later Peter had a prophetic dream. He wrote, *"I was in a large American city and two enormous airplanes appeared over the city, horrible and threatening, and the sky turned dark. A voice inside me said that these airplanes were going to attack America. They seemed to be passenger aircraft."* (ibid, pages 286-287). This prescient revelation came true within a couple weeks on September 11th.

Mr. Dugulescu concluded, *"I believe that America faces a challenge today more desperate than she has ever experienced before. These times are unique and in times such as this Americans will be those who will decide whether, <u>in the next ten years – or less</u> – American will or will not still be America."* (ibid, page 287; emphasis added). I heard Peter sharing this type of serious warning on several occasions within churches in the USA, just prior to his untimely death. He was a credible voice, and we should take note of his warnings.

On this matter of God's judgment upon His enemies, I wholeheartedly agree with these great men-of-faith – Jonathan Edwards, Leonard Ravenhill, John White, and Peter Dugulescu. All of them acknowledged that judgment is real and hell is a horrible place! It is my belief that if they were still alive they would join me in a chorus of pleading for repentance by anyone and everyone who had ears to hear. The reason is that judgment and hell can be avoided if spiritual leaders would present the whole truth-in-love. Oh – If they would stop serving watered-down milk and baby food to spiritual babies! Oh – If they would just preach the *Whole Counsel of the LORD*! Oh – If they would just call forth disciples of the truth who will genuinely repent of their sin habits and bow the knee!

The American ethicist Helmut Richard Niebuhr wrote about man's tendency to drift toward theological half-truths leads to a compromised message, *"A God without wrath brought men without sin into a kingdom without judgment through the ministrations of a Christ without a cross."* (The Kingdom of God in America; 1939). Ask yourself, hasn't Niebuhr succinctly put his finger on the pulse of comfortable Christianity that is all too common in the West today?

The Lord does not desire for any to perish. He does not delight in the death of the wicked (see Ezekiel 18:23). He is gracious, merciful, and full of compassion. If we will repent, He will relent! He delights in turning His enemies into His children. *"Mercy triumps over judgment"* (James 2:13b). There is no other "god" like Yahweh, who desires to be so personal, intimate, merciful, and forgiving. If we will repent, He will relent! *"Or do you show contempt for the riches of his kindness, tolerance and patience, not realizing that God's kindness leads you toward repentance?"* (Romans 2:4; emphasis added).

GOD'S JUDGMENTS TOWARD HIS CHILDREN

In the other case, which might be harder for some of us to reconcile, God uses adversity and judgments to *discipline* His children. Paul wrote, *"Consider therefore the kindness and sternness of God: sternness to those who fell* [the disbelieving Jews], *but kindness to you* [the engrafted Gentile believers], *provided that you continue in his kindness. Otherwise, you also will be cut off."* (Romans 11:22; emphasis added). God exhibits sternness to those who reject him, but he shows kindness to those who will follow him as His children.

Here the "Heart of the Father" comes through. In God's sovereign plans for His willing followers, He will train, chastise, steer onto the narrow path, restrict opportunities, rebuke, correct, and discipline. These are the behaviors of a loving Father toward His children. A natural benevolent father will not permit his children to be rebellious and run amuck. A natural benevolent father will be not permit his children to pursue everything they desire. He will discipline them for their own good. Now, none of them like it at the time. But eventually those who yield to this "conditioning" will become mature and useful in the Kingdom of God.

Ironically, the discipline is in fact an evidence of the Father's love. *"My son, do not despise the LORD's discipline and do not resent his rebuke, because the LORD disciplines those he loves, as a father the son he delights in."* (Proverbs 3:11-12). This expression of a father's love is elegantly explained in the book of Hebrews,

> *"My son, do not make light of the Lord's discipline, and do not lose heart when he rebukes you, because <u>the Lord disciplines those he loves, and <u>he punishes everyone he accepts as a son</u>."</u> Endure hardship as discipline; God is treating you as sons. For what son is not disciplined by his father? If you are not disciplined (and everyone undergoes discipline), then you are illegitimate children and not true sons. Moreover, we have all had human fathers who disciplined us and we respected them for it. How much more should we submit to the Father of our spirits and live! Our fathers disciplined us for a little while as they thought best; but <u>God disciplines us for our good</u>, that we may share in his holiness. No discipline seems pleasant at the time, but painful. Later on, however, it produces a harvest of righteousness and peace for those who have been trained by it.* (Hebrews 12:5b-11; emphasis added).

I often preach about how God uses the *threshing floor* to *beat the hell out of us*! Just like a farmer forcefully threshing wheat to separate the useful grain from the worthless straw, God strips away and shakes off of us all that is holding us from our past. John-the-baptizer spoke of the Messiah Jesus with these words, *"His winnowing fork is in his hand, and he will clear his threshing floor, gathering his wheat in the barn and burning up the chaff with unquenchable fire."* (Matthew 3:12). Jesus uses evangelists as harvesters to reap the sheaves. And, He uses disciplers as threshers to beat the hell out of believers to transform them into obedient disciples (see 1 Corinthians 9:10-11).

Jesus desires to free us into greater fruitfulness. We need to yield to His sovereign and benevolent hand. He knows what is ultimately best for us. He knows the individual callings and intentions of our lives. He is entitled as our "Father" to discipline us. And, He will use adversity and judgments to accomplish those purposes. Not to destroy us, but to reign us in from waywardness and to sharpen us as weapons for His battles.

Another relevant analogy is that of an owner of a vineyard or orchard who knows that pruning is necessary. One must cut away that which is unproductive or under-productive and draining vital nutrients from being used elsewhere by the rest of the vine or tree. *"He cuts off every branch in me [Jesus] that bears no fruit, while every branch that does bear fruit he prunes so that it will be even more fruitful."* (John 15:2; emphasis added). If we as natural fathers permitted our own children to have their own way -- sleep all day, play all night, party in excess, never work, and show disrespect to those in authority -- wouldn't our children resemble overgrown immature vines or trees that lacked fruit? Fruit comes with maturity. Maturity comes with discipline.

Yet another analogy is that the Holy Spirit metaphorically refines us as precious metal to release from us impurities. Examine the words of Zechariah, *"'In the whole land,' declares the LORD, 'two-thirds will be struck down and perish; yet one-third will be left in it. This third I will bring into the fire: I will refine them like silver and test them like gold. They will call on my name and I will answer them; I will say 'They are my people,' and they will say, 'The Lord is our God.'"* (Zechariah 13:8-9; emphasis added). Note that the majority of the people were struck down and removed, and only one third would remain to be refined as "His own people." Isn't there a relevant parallel today with the majority of so-called "Christians" being in name-only vs. the minority of genuine disciples of Jesus, the latter of whom are defined by their love for Jesus demonstrated through obedience? In this parallel those who are refined by fire are, in fact, His beloved children of His Kingdom.

This concept of God as a benevolent refiner is also presented in the book of Malachi, *"But who can endure the day of his coming? Who can stand when he appears? For he will be like a refiner's fire or a launderer's soap. He will sit as a refiner and purifier of silver; <u>he will purify the Levites and refine them like gold and silver.</u>"* (Malachi 3:2-3a; emphasis added).

This analogy of a refiner is also used by Jeremiah, *"<u>I have made you</u>* [Jeremiah] <u>*a tester of metals and my people the ore,*</u> *that you may observe and test their ways. They are all hardened rebels, going about to slander. They are bronze and iron; they all act corruptly. The bellows blow fiercely to burn away the lead with fire, but the refining goes on in vain; the wicked are not purged out. They are called rejected silver, because the LORD has rejected them."* (Jeremiah 6:27-30; emphasis added). In this latter case, God says that the prophet is the instrument He had chosen to watch and refine the people. Note that some of the corrupt people were so wicked so as to be "beyond" redemption by the refining process.

So, we recognize His benevolent hand at work in each of these four analogies:

- A father disciplining his children
- A farmer threshing his sheaves of grain
- A vineyard owner pruning his vines
- A silversmith or goldsmith refining his precious metals

In all four metaphors the resultant *product* is much more valuable than in its pre-refined state. It has been released from that which kept if from being fully "fruitful" to fulfill it purpose in life. Yet in each case, the object experienced adversity and pain during the transformation.

Adversity has many overlooked benefits. It can serve as a wake up call. It can cause us to face our own humanity, our own vulnerability, and our own mortality. It can humble the self-appointed and the self-exalted. It can give us a second chance to weigh the really important matters of life. It can refocus our attention beyond ourselves. It can stimulate altruism and compassion toward others who are experiencing their own pains.

ADVERSITY FROM THE DEVIL
VS. ADVERSITY FROM GOD

So what are the differences between adversity coming from the devil vs. adversity coming from the LORD, Yahweh? This is a serious and deep question of the motivations between the two sources. Perhaps the following short lists can help bring some level of insight to this perplexing issue. Please consider the following motivations and results as you make a comparison between the two lists:

Adversity from the devil:
- To deceive (see John 8:44)
- To steal, to kill, and to destroy (see John 10:10)
- To stimulate anger, rage, violence
- To stir up rebellion against God and "authority"
- To produce war
- To curse, punish, and produce fear
- To enslave captives
- To cause hopelessness, depravity, and suicide
- To cause physical and mental illness and injury
- To cause chaos
- To exert his authority and dominion on Earth (from the "Second Heaven" realm)
- To disrupt the righteous plans of God
- To demonstrate power and bolster his own false claim to be a supreme "deity"
- To oppose God's prophetic purposes
- To usurp the authority of the Trinity
- To claim his "rights" over his own willing subjects
- To be an accuser of the Brethren of God (e.g., Job)

Adversity from God:

- To judge men according to His righteous standards
- To punish His enemies for rebellion toward His authority
- To permit the consequences of men's sins to be fulfilled (i.e., in connection with the authority already granted to the devil)
- To test, rebuke, correct, discipline, and train His own children as disciples
- To prune away unfruitfulness to yield greater fruitfulness
- To fulfill His prophetic purposes
- To disrupt in order to restore order from chaos
- To judge the devil and his demonic forces
- To produce war for His purposes (e.g., campaigns of Joshua)
- To nourish the earth (e.g., hurricanes and thunderstorms)
- To exert His authority and dominion on Earth (from the "Third Heaven" realm)
- To demonstrate His power (e.g., Moses' prophetic curses in Egypt)
- To stimulate the fear of the LORD
- To dislodge and disrupt the works of the devil
- To redeem mankind by permitting the Messiah to be mocked, rejected, attacked, and crucified

So it isn't a simple matter of "God is a good god" and never engages in adversity. Rather, it is a case of motives and intentions that discriminates between the adversity from the LORD and that from the devil. *"All the ways of the LORD are loving and faithful for those who keep the demands of his covenant."* (Psalm 25:10; emphasis added). Even when God's hand is upon adversity, He remains loving and compassionate and longsuffering. May God Himself give us revelation and greater insight on this matter.

AS WE APPROACH THE END TIMES

God used adversity and judgment in the past in Israel and Judah and against their enemies (some of whom were within Israel and Judah). He is still using these same tools today to the detriment of His enemies and the benefit of His children. *"Jesus Christ is the same yesterday, today, and forever."* (Hebrews 13:8). His character remains the same.

There is yet a day coming when He will judge and rule the nations with a rod of iron. The *Great and Terrible Day of the Lord* is approaching! The *White Throne Judgment* is approaching, when every knee shall bow and every tongue confess that Jesus the Messiah is in fact the Lord God! (see Revelation 20). In the latter days, when darkness reigns upon the earth, there will be "Two Witnesses," prophets of great power and authority raised up by Yahweh (see Revelation 11). These two prophets will bring judgments from their mouths that result in fatalities, adverse weather, and whatever else the Lord desires.

John White wrote, *"You may ask me, 'Are you saying that the church will pass through the Great Tribulation?' I counter, what does it matter? In two-thirds of the world the church is already passing through great tribulation, and she will pass, come what may, through the same here in the West. The point is not will the tribulation be the Tribulation or the great be Great, but will it be or not be? I tell you that unless deep and widespread repentance comes, terrible tribulation will take place in the West."* (*The Golden Cow*, John White, Intervarsity Press, 1979, p. 170).

Leonard Ravenhill wrote, *"Oh that believers would become eternity-conscious! If we could live every moment of every day under the eye of God, if we did every act in the light of the judgment seat, if we sold every article in the light of the judgment seat, if we prayed every prayer in the light of the judgment seat, if we tithed all our possessions in the light of the judgment seat, if we preachers prepared every sermon with one eye on dammed humanity and the other on the judgment seat—then we would have a Holy Ghost revival that would shake this earth and that, in no time at all, would liberate millions of precious souls."* (*Why Revival Tarries*, Leonard Ravenhill, 1987, page 57).

To those among us today who say with confidence that God's judgments were only part of an ancient dispensation for the Hebrews of Israel and Judah and are no longer applicable for today, I have this request. Please honestly consider the following. The Scriptures tell us that God was a judge in *The Beginning* (Genesis) and the He will be a judge in *The End* (Revelation). Yahweh, Who never changes, is *still* a judge at this present time between these two endpoints. That is what is convincingly displayed in the following two chapters. Please read all of the Scriptures carefully, and take the time to meditate on the significance thereof.

6

The God of Adversity in the Old Testament:

Examples of Scripture Indicating that God has an Active Role in Adversity and Judgment

Given the common tendency today for a Christian myopic view of the Bible that only wants to look at passages within the New Testament, we should be aware of the breadth and depth of the invaluable passages of the Old Testament. *"All Scripture is God-breathed and is useful for teaching, rebuking, correcting and training in righteousness…"* (2 Timothy 3:16; emphasis added). Ironically, in the context in which this was written to Timothy, his mentor Paul was referring to the books of the "bible" of his days, the Hebrew Bible (i.e., the Old Testament to Christians). This Hebrew Bible is referred to by the acronym *TaNaKh*, consisting of the Torah (Teachings or Law), the Nevi'im (Prophets), and the Ketuvim (Writings or Wisdom literature). That was the "bible" to Jesus and his early 1st Century followers, such as Paul and Timothy.

As we examine selected Scriptures from the Old Testament (i.e., the Hebrew Bible), please note that the term *LORD* in capital letters denotes *Yahweh* (YHWH) in Hebrew, the specific name of the God of Abraham, Isaac, and Jacob. The alternative term *Lord* has a greater breadth and typically refers to *Adon* in Hebrew, meaning a master, leader, boss, or God. In each passage underlining was included to emphasize where God attributes to Himself active involvement in adversity and judgment.

Now let us consider a subset of the Old Testament explicit examples:

✍ **Genesis 3:16-19**

[16]To the woman <u>he</u> *[the LORD God]* said, "[I] will greatly increase your pains in childbearing; with pain you will give birth to children. Your desire will be for your husband, and he will rule over you." [17]To Adam he said, "Because you listened to your wife and ate from the tree about which I commanded you, 'You must not eat of it,' "Cursed is the ground because of you; through painful toil you will eat of it all the days of your life. [18] It will produce thorns and thistles for you, and you will eat the plants of the field. [19] By the sweat of your brow you will eat your food until you return to the ground, since from it you were taken; for dust you are and to dust you will return."

✍ **Genesis 45:4-8**

[4]Then Joseph said to his brothers, "Come close to me." When they had done so, he said, "I am your brother Joseph, the one you sold into Egypt! [5]And now, do not be distressed and do not be angry with yourselves for selling me here, because it was to save lives that <u>God</u> sent me ahead of you. [6]For two years now there has been famine in the land, and for the next five years there will not be plowing and reaping. [7]But <u>God</u> sent me ahead of you to preserve for you a remnant on earth and to save your lives by a great deliverance. [8]"So then, it was not you who sent me here, but <u>God</u>. He made me father to Pharaoh, lord of his entire household and ruler of all Egypt.

✍ **Genesis 50:18-20**

[18]His brothers then came and threw themselves down before him. "We are your slaves," they said. [19]But Joseph said to them, "Don't be afraid. Am I in the place of God? [20]You intended to harm me, but <u>God</u> intended it for good to accomplish what is now being done, the saving of many lives.

✑ **Exodus 4:6-12**

[6]Then <u>the LORD</u> said, "Put your hand inside your cloak." So Moses put his hand into his cloak, and when he took it out, it was leprous, like snow. [7]"Now put it back into your cloak," he said. So Moses put his hand back into his cloak, and when he took it out, it was restored, like the rest of his flesh. [8]Then the LORD said, "If they do not believe you or pay attention to the first miraculous sign, they may believe the second. [9]But if they do not believe these two signs or listen to you, take some water from the Nile and pour it on the dry ground. The water you take from the river will become blood on the ground." [10]Moses said to the LORD, "O Lord, I have never been eloquent, neither in the past nor since you have spoken to your servant. I am slow of speech and tongue." [11]The LORD said to him, "Who gave man his mouth? Who makes him deaf or mute? Who gives him sight or makes him blind? Is it not <u>I, the LORD</u>? [12]Now go; I will help you speak and will teach you what to say."

[Note: The LORD caused righteous Moses' hand to become leprous. The LORD indicated that He can also make a man deaf, mute, or blind.]

✑ **Exodus 10:27-29**

[27]But <u>the LORD</u> hardened Pharaoh's heart, and he was not willing to let them go. [28]Pharaoh said to Moses, "Get out of my sight! Make sure you do not appear before me again! The day you see my face you will die." [29] "Just as you say," Moses replied, "I will never appear before you again."

✑ **Exodus 12:29-33**

[29]At midnight <u>the LORD</u> struck down all the firstborn in Egypt, from the firstborn of Pharaoh, who sat on the throne, to the firstborn of the prisoner, who was in the dungeon, and the firstborn of all the livestock as well. [30]Pharaoh and all his officials and all the Egyptians got up during the night, and there was loud wailing in Egypt, for there was not a house without someone dead. [31]During the night Pharaoh summoned Moses and Aaron and said, "Up! Leave my people, you and the Israelites! Go,

worship the LORD as you have requested. ³²Take your flocks and herds, as you have said, and go. And also bless me." ³³The Egyptians urged the people to hurry and leave the country. "For otherwise," they said, "we will all die!"

Exodus 15:25-26

²⁵Then Moses cried out to the LORD, and the LORD showed him a piece of wood. He threw it into the water, and the water became sweet. There the LORD made a decree and a law for them, and there <u>he</u> tested them. ²⁶He said, "If you listen carefully to the voice of the LORD your God and do what is right in his eyes, if you pay attention to his commands and keep all his decrees, <u>I</u> will not bring on you any of the diseases <u>I</u> brought on the Egyptians, for I am the LORD, who heals you."

Exodus 23:23

²³<u>My</u> *[God's]* angel will go ahead of you and bring you into the land of the Amorites, Hittites, Perizzites, Canaanites, Hivites and Jebusites, and <u>I</u> will wipe them out.

Exodus 32:25-35

²⁵Moses saw that the people were running wild and that Aaron had let them get out of control and so become a laughingstock to their enemies. ²⁶So he stood at the entrance to the camp and said, "Whoever is for the LORD, come to me." And all the Levites rallied to him. ²⁷Then he said to them, "This is what <u>the LORD</u>, <u>the God of Israel</u>, says: 'Each man strap a sword to his side. Go back and forth through the camp from one end to the other, each killing his brother and friend and neighbor.' " ²⁸The Levites did as Moses commanded, and that day about three thousand of the people died. ²⁹Then Moses said, "You have been set apart to <u>the LORD</u> today, for you were against your own sons and brothers, and he has blessed you this day." ³⁰The next day Moses said to the people, "You have committed a great sin. But now I will go up to the LORD; perhaps I can make atonement for your sin." ³¹So Moses went back to the LORD

and said, "Oh, what a great sin these people have committed! They have made themselves gods of gold. ³²But now, please forgive their sin—but if not, then blot me out of the book you have written." ³³The LORD replied to Moses, "Whoever has sinned against me I will blot out of my book. ³⁴Now go, lead the people to the place I spoke of, and my angel will go before you. However, when the time comes for me to punish, I will punish them for their sin." ³⁵And the LORD struck the people with a plague because of what they did with the calf Aaron had made.

✐ Leviticus 26:14-43

¹⁴But if you will not listen to me and carry out all these commands, ¹⁵and if you reject my decrees and abhor my laws and fail to carry out all my commands and so violate my covenant, ¹⁶then I will do this to you: I will bring upon you sudden terror, wasting diseases and fever that will destroy your sight and drain away your life. You will plant seed in vain, because your enemies will eat it. ¹⁷I will set my face against you so that you will be defeated by your enemies; those who hate you will rule over you, and you will flee even when no one is pursuing you. ¹⁸If after all this you will not listen to me, I will punish you for your sins seven times over. ¹⁹I will break down your stubborn pride and make the sky above you like iron and the ground beneath you like bronze. ²⁰Your strength will be spent in vain, because your soil will not yield its crops, nor will the trees of the land yield their fruit. ²¹If you remain hostile toward me and refuse to listen to me, I will multiply your afflictions seven times over, as your sins deserve. ²²I will send wild animals against you, and they will rob you of your children, destroy your cattle and make you so few in number that your roads will be deserted. ²³If in spite of these things you do not accept my correction but continue to be hostile toward me, ²⁴I myself will be hostile toward you and will afflict you for your sins seven times over. ²⁵And I will bring the sword upon you to avenge the breaking of the covenant. When you withdraw into your cities, I will send a plague among you, and you will be given into enemy hands. ²⁶When I cut off your supply of bread, ten women will be able to bake your bread in one oven, and they will dole out

the bread by weight. You will eat, but you will not be satisfied. [27]If in spite of this you still do not listen to me but continue to be hostile toward me, [28]then in <u>my</u> anger <u>I</u> will be hostile toward you, and <u>I myself</u> will punish you for your sins seven times over. [29]You will eat the flesh of your sons and the flesh of your daughters. [30]<u>I</u> will destroy your high places, cut down your incense altars and pile your dead bodies on the lifeless forms of your idols, and <u>I</u> will abhor you. [31]<u>I</u> will turn your cities into ruins and lay waste your sanctuaries, and I will take no delight in the pleasing aroma of your offerings. [32]<u>I</u> will lay waste the land, so that your enemies who live there will be appalled. [33]<u>I</u> will scatter you among the nations and will draw out <u>my</u> sword and pursue you. Your land will be laid waste, and your cities will lie in ruins. [34]Then the land will enjoy its sabbath years all the time that it lies desolate and you are in the country of your enemies; then the land will rest and enjoy its sabbaths. [35]All the time that it lies desolate, the land will have the rest it did not have during the sabbaths you lived in it. [36]As for those of you who are left, <u>I</u> will make their hearts so fearful in the lands of their enemies that the sound of a windblown leaf will put them to flight. They will run as though fleeing from the sword, and they will fall, even though no one is pursuing them. [37]They will stumble over one another as though fleeing from the sword, even though no one is pursuing them. So you will not be able to stand before your enemies. [38]You will perish among the nations; the land of your enemies will devour you. [39]Those of you who are left will waste away in the lands of their enemies because of their sins; also because of their fathers' sins they will waste away. [40]But if they will confess their sins and the sins of their fathers—their treachery against me and their hostility toward me, [41]which made <u>me</u> hostile toward them so that <u>I</u> sent them into the land of their enemies—then when their uncircumcised hearts are humbled and they pay for their sin, [42]I will remember my covenant with Jacob and my covenant with Isaac and my covenant with Abraham, and I will remember the land. [43]For the land will be deserted by them and will enjoy its sabbaths while it lies desolate without them. They will pay for their sins because they rejected <u>my</u> laws and abhorred <u>my</u> decrees.

✐ **Numbers 12:5a, 9-15**

[5]Then <u>the LORD</u> came down in a pillar of cloud; <u>he</u> stood at the entrance to the Tent and summoned Aaron and Miriam…[9]The anger of <u>the LORD</u> burned against them, and <u>he</u> left them. [10]When the cloud lifted from above the Tent, there stood Miriam—leprous, like snow. Aaron turned toward her and saw that she had leprosy; [11]and he said to Moses, "Please, my lord, do not hold against us the sin we have so foolishly committed. [12]Do not let her be like a stillborn infant coming from its mother's womb with its flesh half eaten away." [13]So Moses cried out to the LORD, "O God, please heal her!" [14]The LORD replied to Moses, "If her father had spit in her face, would she not have been in disgrace for seven days? Confine her outside the camp for seven days; after that she can be brought back." [15]So Miriam was confined outside the camp for seven days, and the people did not move on till she was brought back.

[Note: The LORD caused unrighteous Miriam to become leprous, using the very 'sign' God had demonstrated to Moses in Exodus 4.]

✐ **Deuteronomy 5:8-10**

[8]You shall not make for yourself an idol in the form of anything in heaven above or on the earth beneath or in the waters below. [9]You shall not bow down to them or worship them; for <u>I, the LORD your God</u>, am <u>a jealous God</u>, punishing the children for the sin of the fathers to the third and fourth generation of those who hate <u>me</u>, [10]but showing love to a thousand generations of those who love me and keep my commandments.

✐ **Deuteronomy 7:11-24**

[11]Therefore, take care to follow the commands, decrees and laws I give you today. [12]If you pay attention to these laws and are careful to follow them, then the LORD your God will keep his covenant of love with you, as he swore to your forefathers. [13]He will love you and bless you and increase your numbers. He will bless the fruit of your womb, the crops of your land—your grain, new wine and oil—the calves of your herds and

the lambs of your flocks in the land that he swore to your forefathers to give you. [14]You will be blessed more than any other people; none of your men or women will be childless, nor any of your livestock without young. [15]The LORD will keep you free from every disease. He will not inflict on you the horrible diseases you knew in Egypt, but <u>he</u> will inflict them on all who hate you. [16]You must destroy all the peoples <u>the LORD your God</u> gives over to you. Do not look on them with pity and do not serve their gods, for that will be a snare to you. [17]You may say to yourselves, "These nations are stronger than we are. How can we drive them out?" [18]But do not be afraid of them; remember well what <u>the LORD your God</u> did to Pharaoh and to all Egypt. [19]You saw with your own eyes the great trials, the miraculous signs and wonders, the mighty hand and outstretched arm, with which <u>the LORD your God</u> brought you out. <u>The LORD your God</u> will do the same to all the peoples you now fear. [20]Moreover, <u>the LORD your God</u> will send the hornet among them until even the survivors who hide from you have perished. [21]Do not be terrified by them, for the LORD your God, who is among you, is a great and awesome God. [22]<u>The LORD your God </u>will drive out those nations before you, little by little. You will not be allowed to eliminate them all at once, or the wild animals will multiply around you. [23]But <u>the LORD your God</u> will deliver them over to you, throwing them into great confusion until they are destroyed. [24]<u>He</u> will give their kings into your hand, and you will wipe out their names from under heaven. No one will be able to stand up against you; you will destroy them.

✒ **Deuteronomy 28:15-68**

[15]However, if you do not obey <u>the LORD your God</u> and do not carefully follow all his commands and decrees I am giving you today, all these curses will come upon you and overtake you: [16]You will be cursed in the city and cursed in the country. [17]Your basket and your kneading trough will be cursed. [18]The fruit of your womb will be cursed, and the crops of your land, and the calves of your herds and the lambs of your flocks. [19]You will be cursed when you come in and cursed when you go out.

²⁰The LORD will send on you curses, confusion and rebuke in everything you put your hand to, until you are destroyed and come to sudden ruin because of the evil you have done in forsaking him. ²¹The LORD will plague you with diseases until he has destroyed you from the land you are entering to possess. ²²The LORD will strike you with wasting disease, with fever and inflammation, with scorching heat and drought, with blight and mildew, which will plague you until you perish. ²³The sky over your head will be bronze, the ground beneath you iron. ²⁴The LORD will turn the rain of your country into dust and powder; it will come down from the skies until you are destroyed. ²⁵The LORD will cause you to be defeated before your enemies. You will come at them from one direction but flee from them in seven, and you will become a thing of horror to all the kingdoms on earth. ²⁶Your carcasses will be food for all the birds of the air and the beasts of the earth, and there will be no one to frighten them away. ²⁷The LORD will afflict you with the boils of Egypt and with tumors, festering sores and the itch, from which you cannot be cured. ²⁸The LORD will afflict you with madness, blindness and confusion of mind. ²⁹At midday you will grope about like a blind man in the dark. You will be unsuccessful in everything you do; day after day you will be oppressed and robbed, with no one to rescue you. ³⁰You will be pledged to be married to a woman, but another will take her and ravish her. You will build a house, but you will not live in it. You will plant a vineyard, but you will not even begin to enjoy its fruit. ³¹Your ox will be slaughtered before your eyes, but you will eat none of it. Your donkey will be forcibly taken from you and will not be returned. Your sheep will be given to your enemies, and no one will rescue them. ³²Your sons and daughters will be given to another nation, and you will wear out your eyes watching for them day after day, powerless to lift a hand. ³³A people that you do not know will eat what your land and labor produce, and you will have nothing but cruel oppression all your days. ³⁴The sights you see will drive you mad. ³⁵The LORD will afflict your knees and legs with painful boils that cannot be cured, spreading from the soles of your feet to the top of your head. ³⁶The LORD will drive you and the king you set over you to a nation unknown to you or your fathers. There you will worship other gods, gods of wood

and stone. ³⁷You will become a thing of horror and an object of scorn and ridicule to all the nations where <u>the LORD</u> will drive you. ³⁸You will sow much seed in the field but you will harvest little, because locusts will devour it. ³⁹You will plant vineyards and cultivate them but you will not drink the wine or gather the grapes, because worms will eat them. ⁴⁰You will have olive trees throughout your country but you will not use the oil, because the olives will drop off. ⁴¹You will have sons and daughters but you will not keep them, because they will go into captivity. ⁴²Swarms of locusts will take over all your trees and the crops of your land. ⁴³The alien who lives among you will rise above you higher and higher, but you will sink lower and lower. ⁴⁴He will lend to you, but you will not lend to him. He will be the head, but you will be the tail. ⁴⁵All these curses will come upon you. They will pursue you and overtake you until you are destroyed, because you did not obey <u>the LORD your God</u> and observe the commands and decrees <u>he</u> gave you. ⁴⁶They will be a sign and a wonder to you and your descendants forever. ⁴⁷Because you did not serve <u>the LORD your God</u> joyfully and gladly in the time of prosperity, ⁴⁸therefore in hunger and thirst, in nakedness and dire poverty, you will serve the enemies <u>the LORD</u> sends against you. <u>He</u> will put an iron yoke on your neck until <u>he</u> has destroyed you. ⁴⁹<u>The LORD</u> will bring a nation against you from far away, from the ends of the earth, like an eagle swooping down, a nation whose language you will not understand, ⁵⁰a fierce-looking nation without respect for the old or pity for the young. ⁵¹They will devour the young of your livestock and the crops of your land until you are destroyed. They will leave you no grain, new wine or oil, nor any calves of your herds or lambs of your flocks until you are ruined. ⁵²They will lay siege to all the cities throughout your land until the high fortified walls in which you trust fall down. They will besiege all the cities throughout the land the LORD your God is giving you. ⁵³Because of the suffering that your enemy will inflict on you during the siege, you will eat the fruit of the womb, the flesh of the sons and daughters the LORD your God has given you. ⁵⁴Even the most gentle and sensitive man among you will have no compassion on his own brother or the wife he loves or his surviving children, ⁵⁵and he will not give to one of them any of the flesh of his children that he is eating. It will be all he has left because of the suffering your enemy will inflict on you during the siege of all your cities. [56]The most gentle and sensitive woman among you—so sensitive and gentle that she would not venture to touch the ground with the sole of her foot—will begrudge the husband she loves and her own son or daughter the [57]afterbirth from her womb and the children she bears. For she intends to eat them secretly during the siege and in the distress that your enemy will inflict on you in your cities. [58]If you do not carefully follow all the words of this law, which are written in this book, and do not revere this glorious and awesome name—the LORD your God—[59]the LORD will send fearful plagues on you and your descendants, harsh and prolonged disasters, and severe and lingering illnesses. [60]He will bring upon you all the diseases of Egypt that you dreaded, and they will cling to you. [61]The LORD will also bring on you every kind of sickness and disaster not recorded in this Book of the Law, until you are destroyed. [62]You who were as numerous as the stars in the sky will be left but few in number, because you did not obey the LORD your God. [63]Just as it pleased the LORD to make you prosper and increase in number, so it will please him to ruin and destroy you. You will be uprooted from the land you are entering to possess. [64]Then the LORD will scatter you among all nations, from one end of the earth to the other. There you will worship other gods—gods of wood and stone, which neither you nor your fathers have known. [65]Among those nations you will find no repose, no resting place for the sole of your foot. There the LORD will give you an anxious mind, eyes weary with longing, and a despairing heart. [66]You will live in constant suspense, filled with dread both night and day, never sure of your life. [67]In the morning you will say, "If only it were evening!" and in the evening, "If only it were morning!"—because of the terror that will fill your hearts and the sights that your eyes will see. [68]The LORD will send you back in ships to Egypt on a journey I said you should never make again. There you will offer yourselves for sale to your enemies as male and female slaves, but no one will buy you.

ᔈ **Deuteronomy 32:39-43**

39"See now that I myself am He! There is no god besides me. I put to
death and I bring to life, I have wounded and I will heal, and no one can
deliver out of my hand. 40I lift my hand to heaven and declare: As surely
as I live forever, 41when I sharpen my flashing sword and my hand grasps
it in judgment, I will take vengeance on my adversaries and repay those
who hate me. 42I will make my arrows drunk with blood, while my sword
devours flesh: the blood of the slain and the captives, the heads of the
enemy leaders." 43Rejoice, O nations, with his people, for he will avenge
the blood of his servants; he will take vengeance on his enemies and make
atonement for his land and people.

ᔈ **1 Samuel 2:6-10**

6The LORD brings death and makes alive; he brings down to the
grave and raises up. 7The LORD sends poverty and wealth; he humbles
and he exalts. 8He raises the poor from the dust and lifts the needy from
the ash heap; he seats them with princes and has them inherit a throne
of honor. For the foundations of the earth are the LORD's; upon them
he has set the world. 9He will guard the feet of his saints, but the wicked
will be silenced in darkness. "It is not by strength that one prevails; 10those
who oppose the LORD will be shattered. He will thunder against them
from heaven; the LORD will judge the ends of the earth. He will give
strength to his king and exalt the horn of his anointed."

ᔈ **1Samuel 16:14-15**

14Now the Spirit of the LORD had departed from Saul, and an evil
spirit from the LORD tormented him. 15Saul's attendants said to him,
"See, an evil spirit from God is tormenting you."

ᔈ **1 Samuel 25:36-39**

36When Abigail went to Nabal, he was in the house holding a banquet
like that of a king. He was in high spirits and very drunk. So she told

him nothing until daybreak. ³⁷Then in the morning, when Nabal was sober, his wife told him all these things, and his heart failed him and he became like a stone. ³⁸About ten days later, the LORD struck Nabal and he died. ³⁹When David heard that Nabal was dead, he said, "Praise be to the LORD, who has upheld my cause against Nabal for treating me with contempt. He has kept his servant from doing wrong and has brought Nabal's wrongdoing down on his own head."

✐ 2 Samuel 3:28-30

²⁸Later, when David heard about this, he said, "I and my kingdom are forever innocent before the LORD concerning the blood of Abner son of Ner. ²⁹May his blood fall upon the head of Joab and upon all his father's house! May Joab's house never be without someone who has a running sore or leprosy or who leans on a crutch or who falls by the sword or who lacks food." ³⁰(Joab and his brother Abishai murdered Abner because he had killed their brother Asahel in the battle at Gibeon.)

[Note: Righteous David pronounced a curse upon unrighteous Joab's family line.]

✐ 2 Samuel 12:13-18a

¹³Then David said to Nathan, "I have sinned against the LORD." Nathan replied, "The LORD has taken away your sin. You are not going to die. ¹⁴But because by doing this you have made the enemies of the LORD show utter contempt, the son born to you will die." ¹⁵After Nathan had gone home, the LORD struck the child that Uriah's wife had borne to David, and he became ill. ¹⁶David pleaded with God for the child. He fasted and went into his house and spent the nights lying on the ground. ¹⁷The elders of his household stood beside him to get him up from the ground, but he refused, and he would not eat any food with them. ¹⁸On the seventh day the child died...

✑ 2 Kings 5:25-27

²⁵Then he went in and stood before his master Elisha. "Where have you been, Gehazi?" Elisha asked. "Your servant didn't go anywhere," Gehazi answered. ²⁶But Elisha said to him, "Was not my spirit with you when the man got down from his chariot to meet you? Is this the time to take money, or to accept clothes, olive groves, vineyards, flocks, herds, or menservants and maidservants? ²⁷Naaman's leprosy will cling to you and to your descendants forever." Then Gehazi went from Elisha's presence and he was leprous, as white as snow.

[Note: This is reminiscent of Miriam's leprosy caused by her disobedience in Numbers 12, for envy and contempt toward the righteous prophet Moses. Likewise, Gehazi and his descendents were afflicted with leprosy for greed and contempt concerning the affairs of the righteous prophet Elisha.]

✑ 1 Chronicles 16:14, 25, 30, 33

¹⁴<u>He</u> is <u>the LORD</u> our <u>God</u>; <u>his</u> judgments are in all the earth…²⁵For great is <u>the LORD</u> and most worthy of praise; <u>he</u> is to be feared above all gods…³⁰Tremble before <u>him</u>, all the earth! The world is firmly established; it cannot be moved…³³Then the trees of the forest will sing, they will sing for joy before <u>the LORD</u>, for <u>he</u> comes to judge the earth.

✑ 1 Chronicles 21:9-19

⁹The LORD said to Gad, David's seer, ¹⁰"Go and tell David, 'This is what <u>the LORD</u> says: <u>I</u> am giving you three options. Choose one of them for <u>me</u> to carry out against you.'" ¹¹So Gad went to David and said to him, "This is what <u>the LORD</u> says: 'Take your choice: ¹²three years of famine, three months of being swept away before your enemies, with their swords overtaking you, or three days of the sword of <u>the LORD</u>—days of plague in the land, with the angel of <u>the LORD</u> ravaging every part of Israel.' Now then, decide how I should answer the one who sent me." ¹³David said to Gad, "I am in deep distress. Let me fall into the hands of the LORD, for his mercy is very great; but do not let me fall into the hands of

men." ¹⁴So <u>the LORD</u> sent a plague on Israel, and seventy thousand men of Israel fell dead. ¹⁵And <u>God</u> sent an angel to destroy Jerusalem. But as the angel was doing so, the LORD saw it and was grieved because of the calamity and said to the angel who was destroying the people, "Enough! Withdraw your hand." The angel of <u>the LORD</u> was then standing at the threshing floor of Araunah the Jebusite. ¹⁶David looked up and saw the angel of <u>the LORD</u> standing between heaven and earth, with a drawn sword in his hand extended over Jerusalem. Then David and the elders, clothed in sackcloth, fell facedown. ¹⁷David said to God, "Was it not I who ordered the fighting men to be counted? I am the one who has sinned and done wrong. These are but sheep. What have they done? O <u>LORD my God</u>, let your hand fall upon me and my family, but do not let this plague remain on your people." ¹⁸Then the angel of the LORD ordered Gad to tell David to go up and build an altar to the LORD on the threshing floor of Araunah the Jebusite. ¹⁹So David went up in obedience to the word that Gad had spoken in the name of the LORD.

✑ 2 Chronicles 7:13-14

¹³When <u>I</u> shut up the heavens so that there is no rain, or command locusts to devour the land or send a plague among my people, ¹⁴if my people, who are called by my name, will humble themselves and pray and seek my face and turn from their wicked ways, then will I hear from heaven and will forgive their sin and will heal their land.

✑ 2 Kings 20:12-19

¹²At that time Merodach-Baladan son of Baladan king of Babylon sent Hezekiah letters and a gift, because he had heard of Hezekiah's illness. ¹³Hezekiah received the messengers and showed them all that was in his storehouses—the silver, the gold, the spices and the fine oil—his armory and everything found among his treasures. There was nothing in his palace or in all his kingdom that Hezekiah did not show them. ¹⁴Then Isaiah the prophet went to King Hezekiah and asked, "What did those men say, and where did they come from?" "From a distant land," Hezekiah replied.

"They came from Babylon." ¹⁵The prophet asked, "What did they see in your palace?" "They saw everything in my palace," Hezekiah said. "There is nothing among my treasures that I did not show them." ¹⁶Then Isaiah said to Hezekiah, "Hear the word of <u>the LORD</u>: ¹⁷The time will surely come when everything in your palace, and all that your fathers have stored up until this day, will be carried off to Babylon. Nothing will be left, says <u>the LORD</u>. ¹⁸And some of your descendants, your own flesh and blood, that will be born to you, will be taken away, and they will become eunuchs in the palace of the king of Babylon." ¹⁹"The word of the LORD you have spoken is good," Hezekiah replied. For he thought, "Will there not be peace and security in my lifetime?"

[Note: Because of King Hezekiah's sin, the LORD said that He would bring judgment on Hezekiah's descendants and the palace possessions. Hezekiah selfishly preferred his own present comfort at the expense of his future descendants.]

✐ Job 1:8-22

⁸Then <u>the LORD</u> said to Satan, "Have you considered <u>my</u> servant Job? There is no one on earth like him; he is blameless and upright, a man who fears God and shuns evil." ⁹"Does Job fear God for nothing?" Satan replied. ¹⁰"Have you not put a hedge around him and his household and everything he has? You have blessed the work of his hands, so that his flocks and herds are spread throughout the land. ¹¹But stretch out your hand and strike everything he has, and he will surely curse you to your face." ¹²<u>The LORD</u> said to Satan, "Very well, then, everything he has is in your hands, but on the man himself do not lay a finger." Then Satan went out from the presence of the LORD. ¹³One day when Job's sons and daughters were feasting and drinking wine at the oldest brother's house, ¹⁴a messenger came to Job and said, "The oxen were plowing and the donkeys were grazing nearby, ¹⁵and the Sabeans attacked and carried them off. They put the servants to the sword, and I am the only one who has escaped to tell you!" ¹⁶While he was still speaking, another messenger came and said, "The fire of <u>God</u> fell from the sky and burned up the sheep and

the servants, and I am the only one who has escaped to tell you!" ¹⁷While he was still speaking, another messenger came and said, "The Chaldeans formed three raiding parties and swept down on your camels and carried them off. They put the servants to the sword, and I am the only one who has escaped to tell you!" ¹⁸While he was still speaking, yet another messenger came and said, "Your sons and daughters were feasting and drinking wine at the oldest brother's house, ¹⁹when suddenly a mighty wind swept in from the desert and struck the four corners of the house. It collapsed on them and they are dead, and I am the only one who has escaped to tell you!" ²⁰At this, Job got up and tore his robe and shaved his head. Then he fell to the ground in worship ²¹and said: "Naked I came from my mother's womb, and naked I will depart. The LORD gave and <u>the LORD</u> has taken away; may the name of the LORD be praised." ²²In all this, Job did not sin by charging God with wrongdoing.

✍ Job 2:9-10

⁹His wife said to him, "Are you still holding on to your integrity? Curse God and die!" ¹⁰He replied, "You are talking like a foolish woman. Shall we accept good from <u>God</u>, and not trouble?" In all this, Job did not sin in what he said.

✍ Job 13:15

¹⁵Though <u>he</u> slay me, yet will I hope in him; I will surely defend my ways to his face.

✍ Job 42:10-11

After Job had prayed for his friends, the LORD made him prosperous again and gave him twice as much as he had before. ¹¹All his brothers and sisters and everyone who had known him before came and ate with him in his house. They comforted and consoled him over all the trouble <u>the LORD</u> had brought upon him, and each one gave him a piece of silver and a gold ring.

✍ **Psalm 2:10-12**

¹⁰Therefore, you kings, be wise; be warned, you rulers of the earth. ¹¹Serve <u>the LORD</u> with fear and rejoice with trembling. ¹²Kiss <u>the Son</u>, lest <u>he</u> be angry and you be destroyed in your way, for <u>his</u> wrath can flare up in a moment. Blessed are all who take refuge in him.

✍ **Psalm 18:7-14**

⁷The earth trembled and quaked, and the foundations of the mountains shook; they trembled because <u>he</u> was angry. ⁸Smoke rose from <u>his</u> nostrils; consuming fire came from <u>his</u> mouth, burning coals blazed out of it. ⁹<u>He</u> parted the heavens and came down; dark clouds were under <u>his</u> feet. ¹⁰<u>He</u> mounted the cherubim and flew; <u>he</u> soared on the wings of the wind. ¹¹<u>He</u> made darkness <u>his</u> covering, <u>his</u> canopy around <u>him</u>— the dark rain clouds of the sky. ¹²Out of the brightness of <u>his</u> presence clouds advanced, with hailstones and bolts of lightning. ¹³<u>The LORD</u> thundered from heaven; the voice of <u>the Most High</u> resounded. ¹⁴<u>He</u> shot <u>his</u> arrows and scattered the enemies, great bolts of lightning and routed them.

✍ **Psalm 34:19**

¹⁹A righteous man may have many troubles, but the LORD delivers him from them all;

✍ **Psalm 66:10-12**

¹⁰ For <u>you, O God</u>, tested us; <u>you</u> refined us like silver. ¹¹<u>You</u> brought us into prison and laid burdens on our backs. ¹²<u>You</u> let men ride over our heads; we went through fire and water, but you brought us to a place of abundance.

✍ **Psalm 71:20**

²⁰Though <u>you</u> have made me see troubles, many and bitter, you will restore my life again; from the depths of the earth you will again bring me up.

✐ Psalm 76:6-10

⁶At your rebuke, O God of Jacob, both horse and chariot lie still. ⁷You alone are to be feared. Who can stand before you when you are angry? ⁸From heaven you pronounced judgment, and the land feared and was quiet - ⁹when you, O God, rose up to judge, to save all the afflicted of the land. [Selah] ¹⁰Surely your wrath against men brings you praise, and the survivors of your wrath are restrained.

✐ Psalm 78:44-51

⁴⁴He turned their rivers to blood; they could not drink from their streams. ⁴⁵He sent swarms of flies that devoured them, and frogs that devastated them. ⁴⁶He gave their crops to the grasshopper, their produce to the locust. ⁴⁷He destroyed their vines with hail and their sycamore-figs with sleet. ⁴⁸He gave over their cattle to the hail, their livestock to bolts of lightning. ⁴⁹He unleashed against them his hot anger, his wrath, indignation and hostility—a band of destroying angels. ⁵⁰He prepared a path for his anger; he did not spare them from death but gave them over to the plague. ⁵¹He struck down all the firstborn of Egypt, the firstfruits of manhood in the tents of Ham.

✐ Psalm 119:71

⁷¹It was good for me to be afflicted so that I might learn your decrees.

✐ Proverbs 15:25

²⁵The LORD tears down the proud man's house but he keeps the widow's boundaries intact.

✐ Proverbs 16:4

⁴The LORD works out everything for his own ends—even the wicked for a day of disaster.

∽ **Isaiah 10:16-17**

¹⁶Therefore, <u>the Lord, the LORD Almighty</u>, will send a wasting disease upon his *[Assyrian king's]* sturdy warriors; under his pomp a fire will be kindled like a blazing flame. ¹⁷<u>The Light of Israel</u> will become a fire, <u>their Holy One</u> a flame; in a single day it will burn and consume his thorns and his briers.

∽ **Isaiah 19:21-22**

²¹So <u>the LORD</u> will make <u>himself</u> known to the Egyptians, and in that day they will acknowledge <u>the LORD</u>. They will worship with sacrifices and grain offerings; they will make vows to <u>the LORD</u> and keep them. ²²<u>The LORD</u> will strike Egypt with a plague; <u>he</u> will strike them and heal them. They will turn to the LORD, and he will respond to their pleas and heal them.

∽ **Isaiah 30:20-21, 26**

²⁰Although <u>the Lord</u> gives you the bread of adversity and the water of affliction, your teachers will be hidden no more; with your own eyes you will see them. ²¹Whether you turn to the right or to the left, your ears will hear a voice behind you, saying, "This is the way; walk in it." ... ²⁶The moon will shine like the sun, and the sunlight will be seven times brighter, like the light of seven full days, when the LORD binds up the bruises of his people and heals the wounds <u>he</u> inflicted.

∽ **Isaiah 40:1-2**

¹Comfort, comfort my people, says your God. ²Speak tenderly to Jerusalem, and proclaim to her that her hard service has been completed, that her sin has been paid for, that she has received from <u>the LORD'S hand</u> double for all her sins.

∽ **Isaiah 45:7**

⁷<u>I</u> form the light and create darkness, <u>I</u> bring prosperity and create

disaster; <u>I, the LORD</u>, do all these things.

✍ **Isaiah 53:10-11**

[10]Yet it was <u>the LORD's</u> will to crush him *[the Messiah]* and cause him to suffer, and though <u>the LORD</u> makes his life a guilt offering, he will see his offspring and prolong his days, and the will of the LORD will prosper in his hand. [11]After the suffering of his soul, he will see the light of life and be satisfied; by his knowledge my righteous servant will justify many, and he will bear their iniquities.

✍ **Isaiah 54:16-17**

[16]"See, it is <u>I</u> who created the blacksmith who fans the coals into flame and forges a weapon fit for its work. And it is <u>I</u> who have created the destroyer to work havoc; [17]no weapon forged against you will prevail, and you will refute every tongue that accuses you. This is the heritage of the servants of the LORD, and this is their vindication from me," declares <u>the LORD</u>.

✍ **Isaiah 61:1-2**

[1]The Spirit of the Sovereign LORD is on me, because the LORD has anointed me to preach good news to the poor. He has sent me to bind up the brokenhearted, to proclaim freedom for the captives and release from darkness for the prisoners, [2]to proclaim the year of the LORD's favor and the day of vengeance of <u>our God</u>, to comfort all who mourn...

✍ **Isaiah 63:1-6, 10**

[1]Who is this coming from Edom, from Bozrah, with <u>his</u> garments stained crimson? Who is this, robed in splendor, striding forward in the greatness of his strength? "It is <u>I</u>, speaking in righteousness, mighty to save." [2]Why are <u>your</u> garments red, like those of one treading the winepress? [3]"<u>I</u> have trodden the winepress alone; from the nations no one was with <u>me</u>. I trampled them in <u>my</u> anger and trod them down in <u>my</u> wrath; their blood spattered <u>my</u> garments, and <u>I</u> stained all <u>my</u> clothing. [4]For

the day of vengeance was in <u>my</u> heart, and the year of <u>my</u> redemption has come. ⁵<u>I</u> looked, but there was no one to help, <u>I</u> was appalled that no one gave support; so <u>my own</u> arm worked salvation for <u>me</u>, and <u>my own</u> wrath sustained <u>me</u>. ⁶<u>I</u> trampled the nations in <u>my</u> anger; in <u>my</u> wrath <u>I</u> made them drunk and poured their blood on the ground." ... ¹⁰Yet they rebelled and grieved <u>his Holy Spirit</u>. So <u>he</u> turned and became their enemy and <u>he himself</u> fought against them.

✍ Jeremiah 4:11-12

¹¹At that time this people and Jerusalem will be told, "A scorching wind from the barren heights in the desert blows toward <u>my</u> people, but not to winnow or cleanse; ¹²a wind too strong for that comes from <u>me</u>. Now I pronounce <u>my</u> judgments against them."

✍ Jeremiah 32:42-43

⁴²"This is what <u>the LORD</u> says: As <u>I</u> have brought all this great calamity on this people, so I will give them all the prosperity I have promised them. ⁴³Once more fields will be bought in this land of which you say, 'It is a desolate waste, without men or animals, for it has been handed over to the Babylonians.'"

✍ Jeremiah 33:1-6

¹While Jeremiah was still confined in the courtyard of the guard, the word of the LORD came to him a second time: ²"This is what the LORD says, he who made the earth, the LORD who formed it and established it—the LORD is his name: ³'Call to me and I will answer you and tell you great and unsearchable things you do not know.' ⁴For this is what <u>the LORD, the God of Israel</u>, says about the houses in this city and the royal palaces of Judah that have been torn down to be used against the siege ramps and the sword ⁵in the fight with the Babylonians: 'They will be filled with the dead bodies of the men <u>I</u> will slay in <u>my</u> anger and wrath. I will hide my face from this city because of all its wickedness. ⁶"'Nevertheless, I will bring health and healing to it; I will heal my people and will let

them enjoy abundant peace and security.'"

Lamentations 3:32-39

³²Though <u>he</u> brings grief, he will show compassion, so great is his unfailing love. ³³For he does not willingly bring affliction or grief to the children of men. ³⁴To crush underfoot all prisoners in the land, ³⁵to deny a man his rights before the Most High, ³⁶to deprive a man of justice— would not the Lord see such things? ³⁷Who can speak and have it happen if <u>the Lord</u> has not decreed it? ³⁸Is it not from the mouth of <u>the Most High</u> that both calamities and good things come? ³⁹Why should any living man complain when punished for his sins?

Ezekiel 7:1-9

¹The word of the LORD came to me: ²"Son of man, this is what <u>the Sovereign LORD</u> says to the land of Israel: The end! The end has come upon the four corners of the land. ³The end is now upon you and <u>I</u> will unleash <u>my</u> anger against you. <u>I</u> will judge you according to your conduct and repay you for all your detestable practices. ⁴<u>I</u> will not look on you with pity or spare you; <u>I</u> will surely repay you for your conduct and the detestable practices among you. Then you will know that I am <u>the LORD</u>. ⁵This is what <u>the Sovereign LORD</u> says: Disaster! An unheard-of disaster is coming. ⁶The end has come! The end has come! It has roused itself against you. It has come! ⁷Doom has come upon you—you who dwell in the land. The time has come, the day is near; there is panic, not joy, upon the mountains. ⁸<u>I</u> am about to pour out <u>my</u> wrath on you and spend <u>my</u> anger against you; <u>I</u> will judge you according to your conduct and repay you for all your detestable practices. ⁹<u>I</u> will not look on you with pity or spare you; <u>I</u> will repay you in accordance with your conduct and the detestable practices among you. Then you will know that it is <u>I the LORD</u> who strikes the blow."

Ezekiel 13:8-16

⁸Therefore this is what <u>the Sovereign LORD</u> says: Because of your

false words and lying visions, I am against you, declares the Sovereign LORD. ⁹My hand will be against the prophets who see false visions and utter lying divinations. They will not belong to the council of my people or be listed in the records of the house of Israel, nor will they enter the land of Israel. Then you will know that I am the Sovereign LORD. ¹⁰Because they lead my people astray, saying, "Peace," when there is no peace, and because, when a flimsy wall is built, they cover it with whitewash, ¹¹therefore tell those who cover it with whitewash that it is going to fall. Rain will come in torrents, and I will send hailstones hurtling down, and violent winds will burst forth. ¹²When the wall collapses, will people not ask you, "Where is the whitewash you covered it with?" ¹³Therefore this is what the Sovereign LORD says: In my wrath I will unleash a violent wind, and in my anger hailstones and torrents of rain will fall with destructive fury. ¹⁴I will tear down the wall you have covered with whitewash and will level it to the ground so that its foundation will be laid bare. When it falls, you will be destroyed in it; and you will know that I am the LORD. ¹⁵So I will spend my wrath against the wall and against those who covered it with whitewash. I will say to you, "The wall is gone and so are those who whitewashed it, ¹⁶those prophets of Israel who prophesied to Jerusalem and saw visions of peace for her when there was no peace, declares the Sovereign LORD."

∂ Ezekiel 15:6-8

⁶Therefore this is what the Sovereign LORD says: As I have given the wood of the vine among the trees of the forest as fuel for the fire, so will I treat the people living in Jerusalem. ⁷I will set my face against them. Although they have come out of the fire, the fire will yet consume them. And when I set my face against them, you will know that I am the LORD. ⁸I will make the land desolate because they have been unfaithful, declares the Sovereign LORD."

∂ Ezekiel 16:49-50

⁴⁹Now this was the sin of your sister Sodom: She and her daughters

were arrogant, overfed and unconcerned; they did not help the poor and needy. ⁵⁰They were haughty and did detestable things before me. Therefore I did away with them as you have seen.

[Note: God describes the sins of Sodom that resulted in its destruction in terms that were broader than sexual depravity alone.]

✐ Ezekiel 20:32-38

³²You say, "We want to be like the nations, like the peoples of the world, who serve wood and stone." But what you have in mind will never happen. ³³As surely as I live, declares <u>the Sovereign LORD</u>, I will rule over you with a mighty hand and an outstretched arm and with outpoured wrath. ³⁴I will bring you from the nations and gather you from the countries where you have been scattered—with a mighty hand and an outstretched arm and with outpoured wrath. ³⁵I will bring you into the desert of the nations and there, face to face, I will execute judgment upon you. ³⁶As I judged your fathers in the desert of the land of Egypt, so I will judge you, declares <u>the Sovereign LORD</u>. ³⁷I will take note of you as you pass under my rod, and I will bring you into the bond of the covenant. ³⁸I will purge you of those who revolt and rebel against <u>me</u>. Although I will bring them out of the land where they are living, yet they will not enter the land of Israel. Then you will know that I am <u>the LORD</u>.

✐ Ezekiel 24:14-18

¹⁴<u>I the LORD</u> have spoken. The time has come for <u>me</u> to act. I will not hold back; I will not have pity, nor will I relent. You will be judged according to your conduct and your actions, declares <u>the Sovereign LORD</u>. ¹⁵The word of <u>the LORD</u> came to me: ¹⁶"Son of man, with one blow I am about to take away from you the delight of your eyes *[his wife]*. Yet do not lament or weep or shed any tears. ¹⁷Groan quietly; do not mourn for the dead. Keep your turban fastened and your sandals on your feet; do not cover the lower part of your face or eat the customary food of mourners ." ¹⁸So I spoke to the people in the morning, and in the evening my wife died. The next morning I did as I had been commanded.

[Note: The LORD killed the righteous prophet's wife as a prophetic sign to the people of Israel.]

Hosea 6:1, 5

¹Come, let us return to the LORD. He has torn us to pieces but he will heal us; he has injured us but he will bind up our wounds... ⁵Therefore I cut you in pieces with my prophets, I killed you with the words of my mouth; my judgments flashed like lightning upon you."

Hosea 9:7-9, 17

⁷The days of punishment are coming, the days of reckoning are at hand. Let Israel know this. Because your sins are so many and your hostility so great, the prophet is considered a fool, the inspired man a maniac. ⁸The prophet, along with my God, is the watchman over Ephraim, yet snares await him on all his paths, and hostility in the house of his God. ⁹They have sunk deep into corruption, as in the days of Gibeah. God will remember their wickedness and punish them for their sins... ¹⁷My God will reject them because they have not obeyed him; they will be wanderers among the nations.

Joel 2:1-2, 25, 30-31

¹Blow the trumpet in Zion; sound the alarm on my holy hill. Let all who live in the land tremble, for the day of the LORD is coming. It is close at hand—²a day of darkness and gloom, a day of clouds and blackness. Like dawn spreading across the mountains a large and mighty army comes, such as never was of old nor ever will be in ages to come... ²⁵I will repay you for the years the locusts have eaten—the great locust and the young locust, the other locusts and the locust swarm—my great army that I sent among you...³⁰I will show wonders in the heavens and on the earth, blood and fire and billows of smoke. ³¹The sun will be turned to darkness and the moon to blood before the coming of the great and dreadful day of the LORD.

✍ **Amos 1:3, 6, 9, 11, 13 and 2:1, 4, 6**

"For three sins of ____ even for four, I will not turn back <u>my</u> wrath."

[Note: This declaration is repeated eight times over different cities and nations.]

✍ **Amos 3:6-7**

⁶When a trumpet sounds in a city, do not the people tremble? When disaster comes to a city, has not <u>the LORD</u> caused it? ⁷Surely <u>the Sovereign LORD</u> does nothing without revealing <u>his</u> plan to <u>his</u> servants the prophets.

✍ **Amos 5:18-20**

¹⁸Woe to you who long for <u>the day of the LORD</u>! Why do you long for <u>the day of the LORD</u>? That day will be darkness, not light. ¹⁹It will be as though a man fled from a lion only to meet a bear, as though he entered his house and rested his hand on the wall only to have a snake bite him. ²⁰Will not <u>the day of the LORD</u> be darkness, not light—pitch-dark, without a ray of brightness?

[Note: The darkness and adversity of "the day of the LORD" is repeated elsewhere, e.g., Joel 2:1-31, Zephaniah 1:14-18, and Malachi 4:1-6.]

✍ **Amos 9:4, 9**

⁴"Though they are driven into exile by their enemies, there <u>I</u> will command the sword to slay them. <u>I</u> will fix my eyes upon them for evil and not for good…⁹For <u>I</u> will give the command, and <u>I</u> will shake the house of Israel among the nations as grain is shaken in a sieve, and not a pebble will reach to the ground."

✍ **Jonah 1:1-4**

¹The word of <u>the LORD</u> came to Jonah son of Amittai: ²"Go to the great city of Nineveh and preach against it, because its wickedness has

come up before me." [3]But Jonah ran away from the LORD and headed for Tarshish. He went down to Joppa, where he found a ship bound for that port. After paying the fare, he went aboard and sailed for Tarshish to flee from the LORD. [4]Then the LORD sent a great wind on the sea, and such a violent storm arose that the ship threatened to break up.

✎ Micah 5:15

[15]"I will take vengeance in anger and wrath upon the nations that have not obeyed me."

✎ Nahum 1:2-6

[2]The LORD is a jealous and avenging God; the LORD takes vengeance and is filled with wrath. The LORD takes vengeance on his foes and maintains his wrath against his enemies. [3]The LORD is slow to anger and great in power; the LORD will not leave the guilty unpunished. His way is in the whirlwind and the storm, and clouds are the dust of his feet. [4]He rebukes the sea and dries it up; he makes all the rivers run dry. Bashan and Carmel wither and the blossoms of Lebanon fade. [5]The mountains quake before him and the hills melt away. The earth trembles at his presence, the world and all who live in it. [6]Who can withstand his indignation? Who can endure his fierce anger? His wrath is poured out like fire; the rocks are shattered before him.

✎ Habbakuk 1:6,12-13

[6]"I am raising up the Babylonians, that ruthless and impetuous people, who sweep across the whole earth to seize dwelling places not their own."…[12]O LORD, are you not from everlasting? My God, my Holy One, we will not die. O LORD, you have appointed them to execute judgment; O Rock, you have ordained them to punish. [13]Your eyes are too pure to look on evil; you cannot tolerate wrong. Why then do you tolerate the treacherous? Why are you silent while the wicked swallow up those more righteous than themselves?

✑ Zephaniah 1:14-18

¹⁴"The great day of the LORD is near—near and coming quickly. Listen! The cry on the day of the LORD will be bitter, the shouting of the warrior there. ¹⁵That day will be a day of wrath, a day of distress and anguish, a day of trouble and ruin, a day of darkness and gloom, a day of clouds and blackness, ¹⁶a day of trumpet and battle cry against the fortified cities and against the corner towers. ¹⁷I will bring distress on the people and they will walk like blind men, because they have sinned against the LORD. Their blood will be poured out like dust and their entrails like filth. ¹⁸Neither their silver nor their gold will be able to save them on the day of the LORD's wrath. In the fire of his jealousy the whole world will be consumed, for he will make a sudden end of all who live in the earth."

✑ Haggai 2:6-8, 16-17

⁶This is what the LORD Almighty says: 'In a little while I will once more shake the heavens and the earth, the sea and the dry land. ⁷I will shake all nations, and the desired of all nations will come, and I will fill this house with glory,' says the LORD Almighty… ¹⁶When anyone came to a heap of twenty measures, there were only ten. When anyone went to a wine vat to draw fifty measures, there were only twenty. ¹⁷I struck all the work of your hands with blight, mildew and hail, yet you did not turn to me,' declares the LORD.

✑ Zechariah 7:8-14

⁸And the word of the LORD came again to Zechariah: ⁹"This is what the LORD Almighty says: 'Administer true justice; show mercy and compassion to one another. ¹⁰Do not oppress the widow or the fatherless, the alien or the poor. In your hearts do not think evil of each other.' ¹¹"But they refused to pay attention; stubbornly they turned their backs and stopped up their ears. ¹²They made their hearts as hard as flint and would not listen to the law or to the words that the LORD Almighty had sent by his Spirit through the earlier prophets. So the LORD Almighty was very angry. ¹³"When I called, they did not listen; so when they called,

I would not listen,' says <u>the LORD Almighty</u>. ¹⁴"<u>I</u> scattered them with a whirlwind among all the nations, where they were strangers. The land was left so desolate behind them that no one could come or go. This is how they made the pleasant land desolate.'"

✐ Zechariah 8:14-15

¹⁴This is what <u>the LORD Almighty</u> says: "Just as <u>I</u> had determined to bring disaster upon you and showed no pity when your fathers angered <u>me</u>," says <u>the LORD Almighty</u>, ¹⁵"so now I have determined to do good again to Jerusalem and Judah. Do not be afraid."

✐ Zechariah 10:1a, 3a

¹Ask the LORD for rain in the springtime; it is <u>the LORD</u> who makes the storm clouds... ³<u>My</u> anger burns against the shepherds, and <u>I</u> will punish the leaders..."

✐ Zechariah 13:8-9

⁸"In the whole land," declares <u>the LORD</u>, "two-thirds will be struck down and perish; yet one-third will be left in it. ⁹This third <u>I</u> will bring into the fire: <u>I</u> will refine them like silver and test them like gold. They will call on my name and I will answer them; I will say 'They are my people,' and they will say, 'The Lord is our God.'"

✐ Zechariah 14:1-2, 16-19

¹A <u>day of the LORD</u> is coming when your plunder will be divided among you. ²<u>I</u> will gather all the nations to Jerusalem to fight against it; the city will be captured, the houses ransacked, and the women raped. Half of the city will go into exile, but the rest of the people will not be taken from the city...¹⁶Then the survivors from all the nations that have attacked Jerusalem will go up year after year to worship the King, the LORD Almighty, and to celebrate the Feast of Tabernacles. ¹⁷If any of the peoples of the earth do not go up to Jerusalem to worship <u>the King</u>, <u>the LORD Almighty</u>, they will have no rain. ¹⁸If the Egyptian people do

not go up and take part, they will have no rain. <u>The LORD</u> will bring on them the plague he inflicts on the nations that do not go up to celebrate the Feast of Tabernacles. ¹⁹This will be the punishment of Egypt and the punishment of all the nations that do not go up to celebrate the Feast of Tabernacles.

✐ Malachi 2:17 – 3:5

¹⁷You have wearied the LORD with your words. "How have we wearied him?" you ask. By saying, "All who do evil are good in the eyes of the LORD, and he is pleased with them" or "Where is the God of justice?" ³:¹"See, <u>I</u> will send my messenger, who will prepare the way before <u>me</u>. Then suddenly <u>the Lord</u> you are seeking will come to <u>his</u> temple; the messenger of the covenant, whom you desire, will come," says <u>the LORD Almighty</u>. ²But who can endure the day of <u>his</u> coming? Who can stand when <u>he</u> appears? For <u>he</u> will be like a refiner's fire or a launderer's soap. ³<u>He</u> will sit as a refiner and purifier of silver; <u>he</u> will purify the Levites and refine them like gold and silver. Then the LORD will have men who will bring offerings in righteousness, ⁴and the offerings of Judah and Jerusalem will be acceptable to the LORD, as in days gone by, as in former years. ⁵"So <u>I</u> will come near to you for judgment. <u>I</u> will be quick to testify against sorcerers, adulterers and perjurers, against those who defraud laborers of their wages, who oppress the widows and the fatherless, and deprive aliens of justice, but do not fear me," says <u>the LORD Almighty</u>.

✐ Malachi 4:1-6

¹"Surely the day is coming; it will burn like a furnace. All the arrogant and every evildoer will be stubble, and that day that is coming will set them on fire," says <u>the LORD Almighty</u>. "Not a root or a branch will be left to them. ²But for you who revere my name, the sun of righteousness will rise with healing in its wings. And you will go out and leap like calves released from the stall. ³Then you will trample down the wicked; they will be ashes under the soles of your feet on the day when <u>I</u> do these things," says <u>the LORD Almighty</u>. ⁴"Remember the law of <u>my</u> servant Moses, the

decrees and laws I gave him at Horeb for all Israel. ⁵"See, I will send you the prophet Elijah before that great and dreadful <u>day of the LORD</u> comes. ⁶He *[the Elijah-like prophet]* will turn the hearts of the fathers to their children, and the hearts of the children to their fathers; or else I will come and strike the land with a curse."

7

The God of Adversity in the New Testament

Examples of Scripture Indicating that God has an Active Role in Adversity and Judgment

✍ Matthew 5:44-45

⁴⁴But I *[Jesus]* tell you: Love your enemies and pray for those who persecute you, ⁴⁵that you may be sons of your Father in heaven. He causes his sun to rise on the evil and the good, and sends rain on the righteous and the unrighteous.

✍ Matthew 10:32-39

³²Whoever acknowledges me *[Jesus]* before men, I will also acknowledge him before my Father in heaven. ³³But whoever disowns me before men, <u>I will disown him before my Father in heaven</u>. ³⁴Do not suppose that I have come to bring peace to the earth. <u>I did not come to bring peace, but a sword</u>. ³⁵ For I have come to turn 'a man against his father, a daughter against her mother, a daughter-in-law against her mother-in-law – ³⁶a man's enemies will be the members of his own household.' ³⁷Anyone who loves his father or mother more than me is not worthy of me; anyone who loves his son or daughter more than me is not worthy of me; ³⁸and anyone who does not take his cross and follow me is not worthy of me. ³⁹Whoever finds his life will lose it, and whoever loses his life for my sake will find it.

✍ **Matthew 11:20-24**

²⁰Then Jesus began to denounce the cities in which most of his miracles had been performed, because they did not repent. ²¹"Woe to you, Korazin! Woe to you, Bethsaida! If the miracles that were performed in you had been performed in Tyre and Sidon, they would have repented long ago in sackcloth and ashes. ²²But I tell you, it will be more bearable for Tyre and Sidon on <u>the day of judgment</u> than for you. ²³And you, Capernaum, will you be lifted up to the skies? No, <u>you will go down to the depths.</u> If the miracles that were performed in you had been performed in Sodom, it would have remained to this day. ²⁴But I tell you that it will be more bearable for Sodom on the <u>day of judgment</u> than for you."

✍ **Matthew 21:18-22**

¹⁸Early in the morning, as he was on his way back to the city, he was hungry. ¹⁹Seeing a fig tree by the road, he went up to it but found nothing on it except leaves. Then he said to it, "<u>May you never bear fruit again!</u>" <u>Immediately the tree withered.</u> ²⁰When the disciples saw this, they were amazed. "How did the fig tree wither so quickly?" they asked. ²¹Jesus replied, "I tell you the truth, if you have faith and do not doubt, not only can you do what was done to the fig tree, but also you can say to this mountain, 'Go, throw yourself into the sea,' and it will be done. ²²If you believe, you will receive whatever you ask for in prayer."

[Note: Jesus <u>cursed</u> an unfruitful fig tree and it died. A parallel passage is in Mark 11.]

✍ **Matthew 23:29-34**

²⁹Woe to you, teachers of the law and Pharisees, you hypocrites! You build tombs for the prophets and decorate the graves of the righteous. ³⁰And you say, 'If we had lived in the days of our forefathers, we would not have taken part with them in shedding the blood of the prophets.' ³¹So you testify against yourselves that you are the descendants of those who murdered the prophets. ³²Fill up, then, the measure of the sin of your

forefathers! ³³You snakes! You brood of vipers! <u>How will you escape being condemned to hell</u>? ³⁴Therefore I am sending you prophets and wise men and teachers. Some of them you will kill and crucify; others you will flog in your synagogues and pursue from town to town.

✐ Matthew 25:31-46

³¹When the Son of Man *[Jesus]* comes in his glory, and all the angels with him, he will sit on his throne in heavenly glory. ³²<u>All the nations will be gathered before him, and he will separate the people one from another as a shepherd separates the sheep from the goats</u>. ³³He will put the sheep on his right and the goats on his left. ³⁴Then the King will say to those on his right, 'Come, you who are blessed by my Father; take your inheritance, the kingdom prepared for you since the creation of the world. ³⁵For I was hungry and you gave me something to eat, I was thirsty and you gave me something to drink, I was a stranger and you invited me in, ³⁶I needed clothes and you clothed me, I was sick and you looked after me, I was in prison and you came to visit me.' ³⁷Then the righteous will answer him, 'Lord, when did we see you hungry and feed you, or thirsty and give you something to drink? ³⁸When did we see you a stranger and invite you in, or needing clothes and clothe you? ³⁹When did we see you sick or in prison and go to visit you?' ⁴⁰The King will reply, 'I tell you the truth, whatever you did for one of the least of these brothers of mine, you did for me.' ⁴¹Then he will say to those on his left, '<u>Depart from me, you who are cursed, into the eternal fire prepared for the devil and his angels</u>. ⁴²For I was hungry and you gave me nothing to eat, I was thirsty and you gave me nothing to drink, ⁴³I was a stranger and you did not invite me in, I needed clothes and you did not clothe me, I was sick and in prison and you did not look after me.' ⁴⁴They also will answer, 'Lord, when did we see you hungry or thirsty or a stranger or needing clothes or sick or in prison, and did not help you?' ⁴⁵He will reply, 'I tell you the truth, whatever you did not do for one of the least of these, you did not do for me.' ⁴⁶Then <u>they will go away to eternal punishment</u>, but the righteous to eternal life.

✍ **Luke 12:4-5**

⁴I *[Jesus]* tell you, my friends, do not be afraid of those who kill the body and after that can do no more. ⁵But I will show you whom you should fear: Fear him *[God]* who, after the killing of the body, <u>has power to throw you into hell</u>. Yes, I tell you, fear him.

✍ **John 3:35-36**

³⁵The Father loves the Son and has placed everything in his hands. ³⁶Whoever believes in the Son has eternal life, but <u>whoever rejects the son will not see life, for God's wrath remains on him.</u>

✍ **John 5:6-9a, 14**

⁶When Jesus saw him *[the paralyzed man]* lying there and learned that he had been in this condition for a long time, he asked him, "Do you want to get well?" ⁷"Sir," the invalid replied, "I have no one to help me into the pool when the water is stirred. While I am trying to get in, someone else goes down ahead of me." ⁸Then Jesus said to him, "Get up! Pick up your mat and walk." ⁹At once the man was cured; he picked up his mat and walked…¹⁴Later Jesus found him at the temple and said to him, "See, you are well again. <u>Stop sinning or something worse may happen to you.</u>"

✍ **John 5:22, 26-30**

²²Moreover, the Father judges no one, but has entrusted <u>all judgment</u> to the Son…²⁶For as the Father has life in himself, so he has granted the Son to have life in himself. ²⁷And he has given him <u>authority to judge</u> because he is the Son of Man. ²⁸Do not be amazed at this, for a time is coming when all who are in their graves will hear his voice ²⁹and come out—those who have done good will rise to live, and <u>those who have done evil will rise to be condemned</u>. ³⁰By myself I can do nothing; <u>I judge only as I hear, and my judgment is just</u>, for I seek not to please myself but him who sent me.

✐ **John 8:11b**

[11]"Then neither do I *[Jesus]* condemn you *[the adulterous woman]*," Jesus declared. "Go now and <u>leave your life of sin</u>."

✐ **John 8:50**

[50]I *[Jesus]* am not seeking glory for myself; but there is one who seeks it, and <u>he</u> *[God]* <u>is the judge</u>.

✐ **John 9:1-7, 35-41**

[1]As he went along, he saw a man blind from birth. [2]His disciples asked him, "Rabbi, who sinned, this man or his parents, that he was born blind?" [3]"Neither this man nor his parents sinned," said Jesus, "<u>but this happened so that the work of God might be displayed in his life</u>. [4]As long as it is day, we must do the work of him who sent me. Night is coming, when no one can work. [5]While I am in the world, I am the light of the world." [6]Having said this, he spit on the ground, made some mud with the saliva, and put it on the man's eyes. [7]"Go," he told him, "wash in the Pool of Siloam" (this word means Sent). So the man went and washed, and came home seeing… [35]Jesus heard that they had thrown him out, and when he found him, he said, "Do you believe in the Son of Man?" [36]"Who is he, sir?" the man asked. "Tell me so that I may believe in him." [37]Jesus said, "You have now seen him; in fact, he is the one speaking with you." [38]Then the man said, "Lord, I believe," and he worshiped him. [39]Jesus said, "<u>For judgment I have come into this world</u>, so that the blind will see and those who see will become blind." [40]Some Pharisees who were with him heard him say this and asked, "What? Are we blind too?" [41]Jesus said, "If you were blind, you would not be guilty of sin; but now that you claim you can see, your guilt remains."

✐ **John 15:1-2**

[1]I *[Jesus]* am the true vine, and <u>my Father</u> is the gardener. [2]He cuts off every branch in me that bears no fruit, while every branch that does bear

~~fruit he prunes~~ so that it will be even more fruitful.

✏ **John 16:32-33**

³²But a time is coming, and has come, when you will be scattered, each to his own home. You will leave me *[Jesus]* all alone. Yet I am not alone, for my Father is with me. ³³I have told you these things, so that in me you may have peace. <u>In this world you will have trouble.</u> But take heart! I have overcome the world.

[Note: See a similar concept in Psalm 34:19.]

✏ **Acts 4:27-29**

²⁷Indeed Herod and Pontius Pilate met together with the Gentiles and the people of Israel in this city to conspire against your holy servant Jesus, whom <u>you</u> anointed. ²⁸<u>They did what your power and will had decided beforehand should happen.</u> ²⁹Now, <u>Lord</u>, consider their threats and enable your servants to speak <u>your</u> word with great boldness.

✏ **Acts 5:1-11**

¹Now a man named Ananias, together with his wife Sapphira, also sold a piece of property. ²With his wife's full knowledge he kept back part of the money for himself, but brought the rest and put it at the apostles' feet. ³Then Peter said, "Ananias, how is it that Satan has so filled your heart that you have lied to the Holy Spirit and have kept for yourself some of the money you received for the land? ⁴Didn't it belong to you before it was sold? And after it was sold, wasn't the money at your disposal? What made you think of doing such a thing? You have not lied to men but to God." ⁵When Ananias heard this, <u>he fell down and died.</u> And great fear seized all who heard what had happened. ⁶Then the young men came forward, wrapped up his body, and carried him out and buried him. ⁷About three hours later his wife came in, not knowing what had happened. ⁸Peter asked her, "Tell me, is this the price you and Ananias got for the land?" "Yes," she said, "that is the price." ⁹Peter said to her, "How could you

agree to test the Spirit of the Lord? Look! The feet of the men who buried your husband are at the door, and they will carry you out also." ¹⁰At that moment <u>she fell down at his feet and died</u>. Then the young men came in and, finding her dead, carried her out and buried her beside her husband. ¹¹Great fear seized the whole church and all who heard about these events.

⸂ Acts 9:15-17

¹⁵But the Lord said to Ananias, "Go! This man *[Saul]* is my chosen instrument to carry my name before the Gentiles and their kings and before the people of Israel. ¹⁶<u>I will show him how much he must suffer for my name</u>." ¹⁷Then Ananias went to the house and entered it. Placing his hands on Saul, he said, "Brother Saul, the Lord—Jesus, who appeared to you on the road as you were coming here—has sent me so that you may see again and be filled with the Holy Spirit."

⸂ Romans 1:18-32

¹⁸<u>The wrath of God</u> is being revealed from heaven against all the godlessness and wickedness of men who suppress the truth by their wickedness, ¹⁹since what may be known about God is plain to them, because God has made it plain to them. ²⁰For since the creation of the world God's invisible qualities—his eternal power and divine nature—have been clearly seen, being understood from what has been made, so that men are without excuse. ²¹For although they knew God, they neither glorified him as God nor gave thanks to him, but their thinking became futile and their foolish hearts were darkened. ²²Although they claimed to be wise, they became fools ²³and exchanged the glory of the immortal God for images made to look like mortal man and birds and animals and reptiles. ²⁴Therefore God gave them over in the sinful desires of their hearts to sexual impurity for the degrading of their bodies with one another. ²⁵They exchanged the truth of God for a lie, and worshiped and served created things rather than the Creator—who is forever praised. Amen. ²⁶Because of this, <u>God gave them over</u> to shameful lusts. Even their women exchanged natural

relations for unnatural ones. ²⁷In the same way the men also abandoned natural relations with women and were inflamed with lust for one another. Men committed indecent acts with other men, and received in themselves the due penalty for their perversion. ²⁸Furthermore, since they did not think it worthwhile to retain the knowledge of God, he gave them over to a depraved mind, to do what ought not to be done. ²⁹They have become filled with every kind of wickedness, evil, greed and depravity. They are full of envy, murder, strife, deceit and malice. They are gossips, ³⁰slanderers, God-haters, insolent, arrogant and boastful; they invent ways of doing evil; they disobey their parents; ³¹they are senseless, faithless, heartless, ruthless. ³²Although they know God's righteous decree that those who do such things deserve death, they not only continue to do these very things but also approve of those who practice them.

[Note: God's wrath can be made manifest by Him giving people over to their sinful demands, so that they reap what they have already sown. Thus, rejecting God's righteous standards results in a lifestyle of overt sin, that is in fact a manifestation of God's wrath.]

Romans 2:1-11

¹You, therefore, have no excuse, you who pass judgment on someone else, for at whatever point you judge the other, you are condemning yourself, because you who pass judgment do the same things. ²Now we know that God's judgment against those who do such things is based on truth. ³So when you, a mere man, pass judgment on them and yet do the same things, do you think you will escape God's judgment? ⁴Or do you show contempt for the riches of his kindness, tolerance and patience, not realizing that God's kindness leads you toward repentance? ⁵But because of your stubbornness and your unrepentant heart, you are storing up wrath against yourself for the day of God's wrath, when his righteous judgment will be revealed. ⁶God "will give to each person according to what he has done." ⁷To those who by persistence in doing good seek glory, honor and immortality, he will give eternal life. ⁸But for those who are self-seeking and who reject the truth and follow evil, there will be wrath and anger.

⁹There will be trouble and distress for every human being who does evil: first for the Jew, then for the Gentile; ¹⁰but glory, honor and peace for everyone who does good: first for the Jew, then for the Gentile. ¹¹For God does not show favoritism.

✒ Romans 5:1-9

¹Therefore, since we have been justified through faith, we have peace with God through our Lord Jesus Christ, ²through whom we have gained access by faith into this grace in which we now stand. And we rejoice in the hope of the glory of God. ³Not only so, but we also rejoice in our sufferings, because we know that suffering produces perseverance; ⁴perseverance, character; and character, hope. ⁵And hope does not disappoint us, because God has poured out his love into our hearts by the Holy Spirit, whom he has given us. ⁶You see, at just the right time, when we were still powerless, Christ died for the ungodly. ⁷Very rarely will anyone die for a righteous man, though for a good man someone might possibly dare to die. ⁸But God demonstrates his own love for us in this: While we were still sinners, Christ died for us. ⁹Since we have now been justified by his blood, how much more shall we be saved from God's wrath through him!

✒ Romans 8:16-18, 28-32

¹⁶The Spirit himself testifies with our spirit that we are God's children. ¹⁷Now if we are children, then we are heirs—heirs of God and co-heirs with Christ, if indeed we share in his sufferings in order that we may also share in his glory. ¹⁸I *[Paul]* consider that our present sufferings are not worth comparing with the glory that will be revealed in us… ²⁸And we know that in all things God works for the good of those who love him, who have been called according to his purpose. ²⁹For those God foreknew he also predestined to be conformed to the likeness of his Son, that he might be the firstborn among many brothers. ³⁰And those he predestined, he also called; those he called, he also justified; those he justified, he also glorified. ³¹What, then, shall we say in response to this? If God is for us, who can be against us? ³²He who did not spare his own Son, but gave him

up for us all—how will he not also, along with him, graciously give us all things? *[Note: See a similar concept to Romans 8:28 in Proverbs 16:4.]*

✑ 1 Corinthians 11:27-32

[27]Therefore, whoever eats the bread or drinks the cup of the Lord in an unworthy manner will be guilty of sinning against the body and blood of the Lord. [28]A man ought to examine himself before he eats of the bread and drinks of the cup. [29]For anyone who eats and drinks without recognizing the body of the Lord eats and drinks judgment on himself. [30]That is why many among you are weak and sick, and a number of you have fallen asleep. [31]But if we judged ourselves, we would not come under judgment. [32]When we are judged by the Lord, we are being disciplined so that we will not be condemned with the world.

✑ 2 Corinthians 5:10-11a

[10]For we must all appear before the judgment seat of Christ, that each one may receive what is due him for the things done while in the body, whether good or bad. [11]Since, then, we know what it is to fear the Lord, we try to persuade men...

✑ 2 Corinthians 6:3-10

[3]We put no stumbling block in anyone's path, so that our ministry will not be discredited. [4]Rather, as servants of God we commend ourselves in every way: in great endurance; in troubles, hardships and distresses; [5]in beatings, imprisonments and riots; in hard work, sleepless nights and hunger; [6]in purity, understanding, patience and kindness; in the Holy Spirit and in sincere love; [7]in truthful speech and in the power of God; with weapons of righteousness in the right hand and in the left; [8]through glory and dishonor, bad report and good report; genuine, yet regarded as impostors; [9]known, yet regarded as unknown; dying, and yet we live on; beaten, and yet not killed; [10]sorrowful, yet always rejoicing; poor, yet making many rich; having nothing, and yet possessing everything.

✍ 2 Corinthians 11:23-31

²³Are they servants of Christ? (I *[Paul]* am out of my mind to talk like this.) I am more. I have worked much harder, been in prison more frequently, been flogged more severely, and been exposed to death again and again. ²⁴Five times I received from the Jews the forty lashes minus one. ²⁵Three times I was beaten with rods, once I was stoned, three times I was shipwrecked, I spent a night and a day in the open sea, ²⁶I have been constantly on the move. I have been in danger from rivers, in danger from bandits, in danger from my own countrymen, in danger from Gentiles; in danger in the city, in danger in the country, in danger at sea; and in danger from false brothers. ²⁷I have labored and toiled and have often gone without sleep; I have known hunger and thirst and have often gone without food; I have been cold and naked. ²⁸Besides everything else, I face daily the pressure of my concern for all the churches. ²⁹Who is weak, and I do not feel weak? Who is led into sin, and I do not inwardly burn? ³⁰If I must boast, I will boast of the things that show my weakness. ³¹The God and Father of the Lord Jesus, who is to be praised forever, knows that I am not lying.

[Note: See Acts 9:16 regarding God's prophetic prediction of Paul's sufferings.]

✍ 2 Corinthians 12:7-10

⁷To keep me from becoming conceited because of these surpassingly great revelations, there was given me a thorn in my flesh, a messenger of Satan, to torment me. ⁸Three times I pleaded with the Lord to take it away from me. ⁹But he said to me, "My grace is sufficient for you, for my power is made perfect in weakness." Therefore <u>I will boast</u> all the more gladly <u>about my weaknesses</u>, so that Christ's power may rest on me. ¹⁰That is why, for Christ's sake, <u>I delight in weaknesses, in insults, in hardships, in persecutions, in difficulties</u>. For when I am weak, then I am strong.

✍ **Galatians 4:13-14**

¹³As you know, it was <u>because of an illness</u> that I *[Paul]* first preached the gospel to you. ¹⁴Even though <u>my illness</u> was a trial to you, you did not treat me with contempt or scorn. Instead, you welcomed me as if I were an angel of God, as if I were Christ Jesus himself.

✍ **Phillipians 1:27-29**

²⁷Whatever happens, conduct yourselves in a manner worthy of the gospel of Christ. Then, whether I *[Paul]* come and see you or only hear about you in my absence, I will know that you stand firm in one spirit, contending as one man for the faith of the gospel ²⁸without being frightened in any way by those who oppose you. This is a sign to them that <u>they will be destroyed</u>, but that you will be saved—and that by God. ²⁹For it has been granted to you on behalf of Christ not only to believe on him, but <u>also to suffer for him</u>, ³⁰since you are going through the same struggle you saw I had, and now hear that I still have.

✍ **Phillipians 2:25-30**

²⁵But I *[Paul]* think it is necessary to send back to you Epaphroditus, my brother, fellow worker and fellow soldier, who is also your messenger, whom you sent to take care of my needs. ²⁶For he longs for all of you and is distressed because you heard <u>he was ill</u>. ²⁷Indeed <u>he was ill, and almost died</u>. But God had mercy on him, and not on him only but also on me, to spare me sorrow upon sorrow. ²⁸Therefore I am all the more eager to send him, so that when you see him again you may be glad and I may have less anxiety. ²⁹Welcome him in the Lord with great joy, and honor men like him, ³⁰because <u>he almost died</u> for the work of Christ, <u>risking his life</u> to make up for the help you could not give me.

✍ **1 Thessalonians 4:3-6**

³It is God's will that you should be sanctified: that you should avoid sexual immorality; ⁴that each of you should learn to control his own body

in a way that is holy and honorable, ⁵not in passionate lust like the heathen, who do not know God; ⁶and that in this matter no one should wrong his brother or take advantage of him. <u>The Lord will punish men for all such sins</u>, as we have already told you and warned you.

✍ 2 Thessalonians 1:6-10

⁶God is just: <u>He will pay back trouble</u> to those who trouble you ⁷and give relief to you who are troubled, and to us as well. This will happen when the Lord Jesus is revealed from heaven in blazing fire with his powerful angels. ⁸<u>He will punish those who do not know God and do not obey the gospel of our Lord Jesus.</u> ⁹<u>They will be punished with everlasting destruction and shut out from the presence of the Lord and from the majesty of his power</u> ¹⁰on the day he comes to be glorified in his holy people and to be marveled at among all those who have believed. This includes you, because you believed our testimony to you.

✍ 2 Thessalonians 2:9-12

⁹The coming of the lawless one will be in accordance with the work of Satan displayed in all kinds of counterfeit miracles, signs and wonders, ¹⁰and in every sort of evil that deceives those who are perishing. <u>They perish because they refused to love the truth</u> and so be saved. ¹¹For this reason <u>God sends them a powerful delusion</u> so that they will believe the lie ¹²and so that all <u>will be condemned</u> who have not believed the truth but have delighted in wickedness.

✍ 1 Timothy 5:23-25

²³Stop drinking only water, and use a little wine <u>because of your stomach and your frequent illnesses.</u> ²⁴The sins of some men are obvious, <u>reaching the place of judgment ahead of them</u>; the sins of others trail behind them. ²⁵In the same way, good deeds are obvious, and even those that are not cannot be hidden.

✐ 2 Timothy 3:1-5

¹But mark this: <u>There will be terrible times in the last days.</u> ²People will be lovers of themselves, lovers of money, boastful, proud, abusive, disobedient to their parents, ungrateful, unholy, ³without love, unforgiving, slanderous, without self-control, brutal, not lovers of the good, ⁴treacherous, rash, conceited, lovers of pleasure rather than lovers of God—⁵having a form of godliness but denying its power. Have nothing to do with them.

✐ 2 Timothy 4:1-3

¹In the presence <u>of God and of Christ Jesus, who will judge the living and the dead,</u> and in view of his appearing and his kingdom, I *[Paul]* give you this charge: ²Preach the Word; be prepared in season and out of season; correct, rebuke and encourage—with great patience and careful instruction. ³For the time will come when men will not put up with sound doctrine. Instead, to suit their own desires, they will gather around them a great number of teachers to say what their itching ears want to hear.

✐ Hebrews 5:7-9

⁷During the days of Jesus' life on earth, he offered up prayers and petitions with loud cries and tears to the one who could save him from death, and he was heard because of his reverent submission. ⁸Although he was a son, he learned obedience from what <u>he suffered</u> ⁹and, once made perfect, he became the source of eternal salvation for all who obey him…

✐ Hebrews 9:27

²⁷Just as man is destined to die once, and after that to face <u>judgment</u>…

✐ Hebrews 10:26-38

²⁶If we deliberately keep on sinning after we have received the knowledge of the truth, no sacrifice for sins is left, ²⁷but only <u>a fearful expectation</u>

of judgment and of raging fire that will consume the enemies of God. [28]Anyone who rejected the law of Moses died without mercy on the testimony of two or three witnesses. [29]How much more severely do you think a man deserves to be punished who has trampled the Son of God under foot, who has treated as an unholy thing the blood of the covenant that sanctified him, and who has insulted the Spirit of grace? [30]For we know him who said, "It is mine to avenge; I will repay," and again, "The Lord will judge his people." [31]It is a dreadful thing to fall into the hands of the living God. [32]Remember those earlier days after you had received the light, when you stood your ground in a great contest in the face of suffering. [33]Sometimes you were publicly exposed to insult and persecution; at other times you stood side by side with those who were so treated. [34]You sympathized with those in prison and joyfully accepted the confiscation of your property, because you knew that you yourselves had better and lasting possessions. [35]So do not throw away your confidence; it will be richly rewarded. [36]You need to persevere so that when you have done the will of God, you will receive what he has promised. [37]For in just a very little while, "He who is coming will come and will not delay. [38]But my righteous one will live by faith. And if he shrinks back, I will not be pleased with him."

✒ Hebrews 12:2-11, 23

[2]Let us fix our eyes on Jesus, the author and perfecter of our faith, who for the joy set before him endured the cross, scorning its shame, and sat down at the right hand of the throne of God. [3]Consider him who endured such opposition from sinful men, so that you will not grow weary and lose heart. [4]In your struggle against sin, you have not yet resisted to the point of shedding your blood. [5]And you have forgotten that word of encouragement that addresses you as sons: "My son, do not make light of the Lord's discipline, and do not lose heart when he rebukes you, [6]because the Lord disciplines those he loves, and he punishes everyone he accepts as a son." [7]Endure hardship as discipline; God is treating you as sons. For what son is not disciplined by his father? [8]If you are not disciplined (and

everyone undergoes discipline), then you are illegitimate children and not true sons. ⁹Moreover, we have all had human fathers who disciplined us and we respected them for it. How much more should we submit to the Father of our spirits and live! ¹⁰Our fathers disciplined us for a little while as they thought best; but <u>God disciplines us for our good</u>, that we may share in his holiness. ¹¹No discipline seems pleasant at the time, but painful. Later on, however, it produces a harvest of righteousness and peace for those who have been trained by it…You have come to God, <u>the judge of all men</u>…

✐ James 1:2-4, 12

²Consider it pure joy, my brothers, <u>whenever you face trials of many kinds</u>, ³because you know that the testing of your faith develops perseverance. ⁴Perseverance must finish its work so that you may be mature and complete, not lacking anything. ¹²Blessed is the man <u>who perseveres under trial</u>, because when he has stood the test, he will receive the crown of life that God has promised to those who love him.

✐ James 5:9-11, 13-16

⁹Don't grumble against each other, brothers, or <u>you will be judged.</u> <u>The Judge is standing at the door!</u> ¹⁰Brothers, as an example of patience in the face of <u>suffering</u>, take the prophets who spoke in the name of the Lord. ¹¹As you know, we consider blessed those who have persevered. You have heard of Job's perseverance and have seen what the Lord finally brought about. The Lord is full of compassion and mercy…¹³Is any one of you in trouble? He should pray. Is anyone happy? Let him sing songs of praise. ¹⁴Is any one of you sick? He should call the elders of the church to pray over him and anoint him with oil in the name of the Lord. ¹⁵And the prayer offered in faith will make the sick person well; the Lord will raise him up. If he has sinned, he will be forgiven. ¹⁶Therefore confess your sins to each other and pray for each other so that you may be healed. The prayer of a righteous man is powerful and effective.

✎ 1 Peter 1:6-7

[6]In this you greatly rejoice, though now for a little while <u>you may have had to suffer grief in all kinds of trials</u>. [7]These have come so that your faith—of greater worth than gold, which perishes even though refined by fire—may be proved genuine and may result in praise, glory and honor when Jesus Christ is revealed.

✎ 1 Peter 4:3-7, 12-19

[3]For you have spent enough time in the past doing what pagans choose to do—living in debauchery, lust, drunkenness, orgies, carousing and detestable idolatry. [4]They think it strange that you do not plunge with them into the same flood of dissipation, and they heap abuse on you. [5]But <u>they will have to give account to him who is ready to judge the living and the dead</u>. [6]For this is the reason the gospel was preached even to those who are now dead, so that they might be judged according to men in regard to the body, but live according to God in regard to the spirit. [7]The end of all things is near. Therefore be clear minded and self-controlled so that you can pray...[12]Dear friends, do not be surprised at the <u>painful trial you are suffering</u>, as though something strange were happening to you. [13]But rejoice that you <u>participate in the sufferings of Christ</u>, so that you may be overjoyed when his glory is revealed. [14]If you are <u>insulted because of the name of Christ</u>, you are blessed, for the Spirit of glory and of God rests on you. [15]If you suffer, it should not be as a murderer or thief or any other kind of criminal, or even as a meddler. [16]However, <u>if you suffer as a Christian</u>, do not be ashamed, but praise God that you bear that name. [17]For it is time <u>for judgment to begin with the family of God</u>; and if it begins with us, what will the outcome be for those who do not obey the gospel of God? [18]And, "If it is hard for the righteous to be saved, what will become of the ungodly and the sinner?" [19]So then, <u>those who suffer according to God's will</u> should commit themselves to their faithful Creator and continue to do good.

[Note: This passage explicitly states that it can be God's will for His followers to suffer.]

1 Peter 5:5-10

⁵Young men, in the same way be submissive to those who are older. All of you, clothe yourselves with humility toward one another, because, "God opposes the proud but gives grace to the humble." ⁶Humble yourselves, therefore, under God's mighty hand, that he may lift you up in due time. ⁷Cast all your anxiety on him because he cares for you. ⁸Be self-controlled and alert. Your enemy the devil prowls around like a roaring lion looking for someone to devour. ⁹Resist him, standing firm in the faith, because you know that your brothers throughout the world are undergoing the same kind of sufferings. ¹⁰And the God of all grace, who called you to his eternal glory in Christ, after you have suffered a little while, will himself restore you and make you strong, firm and steadfast.

2 Peter 2:3-9, 13a, 20-22

³In their greed these *[false prophets and false]* teachers will exploit you with stories they have made up. Their condemnation has long been hanging over them, and their destruction has not been sleeping. ⁴For if God did not spare angels when they sinned, but sent them to hell, putting them into gloomy dungeons to be held for judgment; ⁵if he did not spare the ancient world when he brought the flood on its ungodly people, but protected Noah, a preacher of righteousness, and seven others; ⁶if he condemned the cities of Sodom and Gomorrah by burning them to ashes, and made them an example of what is going to happen to the ungodly; ⁷and if he rescued Lot, a righteous man, who was distressed by the filthy lives of lawless men ⁸(for that righteous man, living among them day after day, was tormented in his righteous soul by the lawless deeds he saw and heard)— ⁹if this is so, then the Lord knows how to rescue godly men from trials and to hold the unrighteous for the day of judgment, while continuing their punishment...¹³They will be paid back with harm for the harm they have done...²⁰If they have escaped the corruption of the world by knowing our Lord and Savior Jesus Christ and are again entangled in it and overcome, they are worse off at the end than they were at the beginning. ²¹It would have been better for them not to have known the way of

righteousness, than to have known it and then to turn their backs on the sacred command that was passed on to them. ²²Of them the proverbs are true: "A dog returns to its vomit," and, "A sow that is washed goes back to her wallowing in the mud."

✐ **Jude 1:14-15**

¹⁴ Enoch, the seventh from Adam, prophesied about these men: "See, the Lord is coming with thousands upon thousands of his holy ones ¹⁵to judge everyone, and to convict all the ungodly of all the ungodly acts they have done in the ungodly way, and of all the harsh words ungodly sinners have spoken against him."

✐ **Revelation 6:9-11**

⁹When he opened the fifth seal, I *[John]* saw under the altar the souls of those who had been slain because of the word of God and the testimony they had maintained. ¹⁰They called out in a loud voice, "How long, Sovereign Lord, holy and true, until you judge the inhabitants of the earth and avenge our blood?" ¹¹Then each of them was given a white robe, and they were told to wait a little longer, until the number of their fellow servants and brothers who were to be killed as they had been was completed.

✐ **Revelation 9:13-21**

¹³The sixth angel sounded his trumpet, and I heard a voice coming from the horns of the golden altar that is before God. ¹⁴It said to the sixth angel who had the trumpet, "Release the four angels who are bound at the great river Euphrates." ¹⁵And the four angels who had been kept ready for this very hour and day and month and year were released to kill a third of mankind. ¹⁶The number of the mounted troops was two hundred million. I heard their number. ¹⁷The horses and riders I saw in my vision looked like this: Their breastplates were fiery red, dark blue, and yellow as sulfur. The heads of the horses resembled the heads of lions, and out of their mouths came fire, smoke and sulfur. ¹⁸A third of mankind was killed by the three plagues of fire, smoke and sulfur that came out of their mouths.

¹⁹The power of the horses was in their mouths and in their tails; for their tails were like snakes, having heads with which they inflict injury. ²⁰The rest of mankind that were not killed by these plagues still did not repent of the work of their hands; they did not stop worshiping demons, and idols of gold, silver, bronze, stone and wood—idols that cannot see or hear or walk. ²¹Nor did they repent of their murders, their magic arts, their sexual immorality or their thefts.

✐ Revelation 11:3-6

³And I will give power to <u>my two witnesses</u>, and they will prophesy for 1,260 days, clothed in sackcloth." ⁴These are the two olive trees and the two lampstands that stand before the Lord of the earth. ⁵If anyone tries to harm them, <u>fire comes from their mouths and devours their enemies</u>. This is how anyone who wants to harm them must die. ⁶These men have power to shut up the sky so that it will not rain during the time they are prophesying; and they have power to turn the waters into blood and to strike the earth with every kind of plague as often as they want.

✐ Revelation 19:11-21

¹¹I saw heaven standing open and there before me was a white horse, whose rider is called Faithful and True. <u>With justice he judges and makes war</u>. ¹²His eyes are like blazing fire, and on his head are many crowns. He has a name written on him that no one knows but he himself. ¹³He is dressed in a robe dipped in blood, and his name is the Word of God. ¹⁴The armies of heaven were following him, riding on white horses and dressed in fine linen, white and clean. ¹⁵Out of his mouth comes a sharp sword with which to strike down the nations. "He will rule them with an iron scepter." He <u>treads the winepress of the fury of the wrath of God Almighty</u>. ¹⁶On his robe and on his thigh he has this name written: KING OF KINGS AND LORD OF LORDS. ¹⁷And I saw an angel standing in the sun, who cried in a loud voice to all the birds flying in midair, "Come, gather together for the great supper of God, ¹⁸so that you may eat the flesh of kings, generals, and mighty men, of horses and their riders, and the

flesh of all people, free and slave, small and great." ¹⁹Then I saw the beast and the kings of the earth and their armies gathered together to make war against the rider on the horse and his army. ²⁰But the beast was captured, and with him the false prophet who had performed the miraculous signs on his behalf. With these signs he had deluded those who had received the mark of the beast and worshiped his image. The two of them were thrown alive into the fiery lake of burning sulfur. ²¹The rest of them were killed with the sword that came out of the mouth of the rider on the horse, and all the birds gorged themselves on their flesh.

[Note: This passage refers to Jesus as one who executes judgment and wrath at the End Times.]

✍ Revelation 20:10-15

¹⁰And the devil, who deceived them, was thrown into the lake of burning sulfur, where the beast and the false prophet had been thrown. They will be tormented day and night forever and ever. ¹¹Then I saw a great white throne and him who was seated on it. Earth and sky fled from his presence, and there was no place for them. ¹²And I saw the dead, great and small, standing before the throne, and books were opened. Another book was opened, which is the book of life. The dead were judged according to what they had done as recorded in the books. ¹³The sea gave up the dead that were in it, and death and Hades gave up the dead that were in them, and each person was judged according to what he had done. ¹⁴Then death and Hades were thrown into the lake of fire. The lake of fire is the second death. ¹⁵If anyone's name was not found written in the book of life, he was thrown into the lake of fire.

RECOMMENDED BOOKS

Praying Faith
Thomas P. Dooley

Hope When Everything Seems Hopeless
Thomas P. Dooley

Repenters
Peter Dugulescu

Revolution
George Barna

Why Revival Tarries
Leonard Ravenhill

Surviving the Anointing:
Learning to Effectively Experience and Walk in God's Power
David Ravenhill

The Golden Cow:
Materialism in the Twentieth-Century Church
John White

Jonathan Edwards: The Great Awakener
Helen K. Hosier

The Problem of Pain
C.S. Lewis

Blue Like Jazz
Don Miller

ABOUT THE AUTHOR

Dr. Tom Dooley is the founder of Path Clearer Inc., a 501(c)(3) organization involved in *Influencing Nations with Truth*. Dr. Dooley is a prophetic preacher among the nations, and the author of **Praying Faith** and **Hope When Everything Seems Hopeless**. Tom has a diverse professional background and has been active in various ministries. From humble beginnings as a boy on a Kansas farm, he subsequently became a research scientist, professor, and entrepreneur. Tom has a Ph.D. in molecular biology and has worked for two decades in drug discovery and development in the pharmaceutical industry and in academia. Furthermore, Dr. Tom Dooley is a serial entrepreneur, having founded various companies and nonprofit organizations. He is an advocate for *bi-vocational ministry in the marketplace 24/7,* or in other words advancing the Kingdom of God beyond the walls of the local church. Dr. Dooley has a diverse set of perspectives seldom provided by other authors. He addresses issues from a Biblical worldview and firsthand remarkable testimonies of faith. He has had influence from the pauper to the President. Tom has been married for more than a quarter century to his loving and precious wife, Laura. They have four children and one daughter-in-law.

CONTACT THE AUTHOR

info@pathclearer.com

www.pathclearer.com

Path Clearer, Inc.

PO Box 661466

Birmingham, Alabama

35266-1466 USA